D1311096

Dany Sautot

the story of
Baccarat...

1764 →

Collection directed by

Fabienne de Seze

Curator of the

Baccarat Museums

Published by Baccarat - **1993**

The Sainte-Anne glassworks at Baccarat

D'Artigues: the Vonêche crystalworks at Baccarat

From the Restoration to the July Monarchy: the premises of fame

Watchword: perfection

- Louix XVIII
- Hot-work process
- Cold-work process
- First products
- Lighting fixtures
- Competition
- Charles X
- Louis - Philippe
- Launay, Hautin & Cie (1832-1857)
- New processes - new products
- François-Eugène de Fontenay (1810-1884)
- On the perfection of clear crystal
- From the colors of crystal to agate glass
- "Millefiori"
- "Sulphide" paperweights

Baccarat during the 1848 unrest

From renown to supremacy: the splendor of the Second Empire

1855-1867: from one Great Exhibition to the next

- Siemens furnace
- From wheel-engraving to acid-etched engraving: the Kessler process
- Crucibles
- Baccarat: the first signature...
- Baccarat on the Champs de Mars: the 1867 World's Fair

1867-1870: the end of the "Imperial Feast"

The Republi settles in...

- Paris, 1878: The World's Fair
- 1889-1900: Baccar statement on social policy

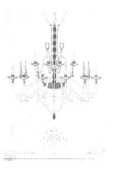

Baccarat Museum

30 bis rue de Paradis

75010 Paris

Baccarat Museum

54120 Baccarat

BACCARAT [bakaʀa]. *n.m.* **(1898 ; from** *Baccarat,* **town).**

Crystalware from the Baccarat factory. *Baccarat glasses.*

Trans. **Petit Robert,** dictionnaire de la langue française

Thus, in 1898, the name of Baccarat, a small town in Lorraine, on the slope of
the Vosges mountains and the banks of the river Meurthe, about twenty-five miles from
Nancy, became synonymous with one of France's most prestigious products: Baccarat
crystalware.

Who were the main protagonists who contributed to its reputation, from the eve of
the French Revolution up until the dawn of the twenty-first century?

How did Baccarat adapt to the events of such a tumultuous period of history between
changing political climates, the great industrial and social upheavals of the nineteenth
century and the new socio-economic circumstances of the twentieth century?

Why is Baccarat, a pioneer industry, also steeped in tradition? To these numerous
questions, the rich industrial heritage scrupulously preserved by the glassworks provides
some answers.

Consulting the annual reports of the Glassworks' Board of Directors going back to 1823,
as well as the order books and catalogues has given an insight into the Company's past.
Thanks to the detailed archives kept in the Drawings Room and the objects stored in the
various stockrooms, the Company's two museums were set up on sites closely linked to
its history. The first is in the town of Baccarat, opposite the halle (workshop), in the
director's former residence, called the "Château," bordered on both sides by the
glassmakers' quarters. The other is in Paris in an old post house which used to
accommodate travelers from eastern France and which became the Glassworks'
storehouse during the nineteenth century.

Fabienne de Seze, Curator of the Baccarat Museums

Crystal palaces along the paths

traveled by the Knights

of the Holy Grail...

Crystal balls that reveal the future...

Rock crystal...

Venetian crystal...

Bohemian crystal...

Crystal glass...

Crystal...

Ambiguous, mythical term,

made complex by its image,

forever reflected

from the imaginary world to reality.

Crystal?

Under the 1971 order covering the whole of the European Community, the term "crystal" refers to a glass with a refractory index equal to or greater than 1.545. This very accurate figure is the result of lengthy research made up of a good deal of trial and error, and adventures punctuated by coincidences, exchanges and the inventive spirit of glassmakers.

It was seemingly during the second half of the fifteenth century that the Venetians started producing a particularly fine glass whose transparency was redolent of rock crystal. This glass, called *cristallo*, testifies to the extraordinary level of knowledge and technical expertise achieved by Venetian glassmakers living on the island of Murano from the end of the thirteenth century. Made from very costly raw materials such as soda imported from Spain, *cristallo* was used to create luxurious pieces intended for a very wealthy clientele. This type of glass was perfected during the sixteenth century, enriched with new decoration (diamond-point engraving, enamelled motifs, gilding, blue glass handles attached using a hot work process) and bold shapes made possible by its great malleability due to the high soda content. Until the end of the seventeenth century, Venice and its glassmakers had supremacy over the world's luxury glassware market. Despite the drastic orders prohibiting Venetian glassmakers from leaving the country during the sixteenth and the seventeenth centuries many of them emigrated, mainly to England, France and the Netherlands, but also to Germanic nations and the countries of central Europe. In their new homelands, they created production centers, making a type of glassware known as *"façon de Venise"* ("in the Venetian manner") popular with a well-off clientele.

Bohemia was also influenced by the Venetian glassmakers who settled there after 1557. However, the difficulties encountered in finding soda supplies forced the glassmakers to use an improved version of the traditional compound for making Bohemian glass, a potash-based product extracted from wood ashes.

This produced a less malleable paste which limited the range of shapes; the glass obtained lacked the refinement and clarity of *cristallo*. On account of its hardness, this glass was nevertheless eminently suitable for diamond-point engraving. When, in 1600, Rudolf the Second (1576-1612), Emperor of the Holy Roman Empire, set up court in Prague, he attracted numerous artists and a large intellectual elite. Around the imperial patron, the town became an artistic center where Mannerism flourished. The vogue for cut and engraved precious stones and rock crystal paved the way for applying glyptic techniques (the art of engraving on semi-precious stones) to glass.

When the term *Bohemian crystal* appeared during the second half of the seventeenth century, it completed the progress achieved in obtaining glass comparable to rock-crystal, not only for its clarity but for its hardness and brilliance. A thoroughly organized commercial network helped this glass acquire a worldwide reputation, and during the eighteenth century, it supplanted Venetian glassware.

However, it is neither to the Venetian glassmakers nor to their Bohemian counterparts that we owe the discovery of lead crystal, the only kind which met the famous 1.545 refractive index. Its origins date back to seventeenth century England. When, in 1615, King James Ist reserved the exploitation of forests to the shipyards and forbade the use of wood as fuel, glassmakers were forced to replace it with coal. Previously, raw materials were fused in open crucibles, but the chemical reactions triggered between combustion gas and the batch colored the glass. The crucibles were then covered in order to isolate and protect the fusion process. With this new process, fusibility problems arose which forced glassmakers to reconsider the proportions of raw materials. In 1676, after various experiments, glass industrialist George Ravenscroft had the idea of adding lead oxide (minium or red lead) as a mineral flux to the initial compound. Even though it did not have the clarity, sparkle, whiteness and sound which characterize it today, lead crystal was born. From the end of the seventeenth century onwards, and during the eighteenth century, it would be improved considerably by processes providing increasingly purified raw materials: calcinating and washing potash, selecting the whitest sands, producing minium with the best-quality lead, etc. New shapes were created around this new material which could not be worked in the *"Venetian manner"*. Since they were heavier, the glasses often had a baluster stem with one or more lumps and sometimes an air bubble trapped inside. The base was round and dome-shaped. Everything was done intentionally to let the light "play" inside the dazzling new material. When William of Orange, Governor of the Netherlands, became King of England, in 1688, close ties were forged between the two countries. British glassmakers then exported their raw crystal which was engraved in the Netherlands, where a new technique was developed called stippled engraving. This method was the source for the reputation enjoyed by Dutch engraved glassware. The success of British crystal spread throughout Europe, North America and India. The shapes evolved, and during the second half of the eighteenth century, glasses appeared with a funneled bowl, connected to a solid base by a straight stem. 1760 marked the appearance of the first English wheel-engraved glasses. At first, the engravings were simple facets on the stem; then they became deeper and more intricate. Crystal light fixtures were launched at the same time. A new *art de vivre* was born. The dark interiors of homes gave way to the sparkling light of chandeliers, streaming with engraved crystal pendants reflecting ad infinitum the dancing flames of the candles. Despite the continuous conflicts which divided the French and the English, France was consistently struck by Anglomania. Thus, the French attempted to imitate English crystal, which glass-lovers bought in specialty shops such as Le Petit Dunkerque, in Paris. The first French crystalware was soon compared to its English counterpart.

After a number of unsuccessful attempts, the first French lead crystal glasses appeared in 1781. They were comparable in all respects to the glassware from across the Channel. However, the economic slump which had paralyzed France since 1770 and the Revolution which ensued did little to encourage this nascent industry. It was not until the beginning of the nineteenth century that it would genuinely blossom.

the story of
Baccarat,

1764 →

Baccarat Crystalworks

1837

Louis de Montmorency-Laval

The Sainte-Anne Glassworks at Baccarat

1764 - 1816

Until 1760, the Baccarat *châtellenie*, temporal property of the Bishopric of Metz, lived off its forestry. A large population of lumberjacks exploited the forest. Most of the wood was used to supply the furnaces of the Rosières saltworks. Twice a year, during high water in the spring and in the fall, tree trunks were thrown into the Meurthe river. An army of day laborers equipped with pikes channeled them from the banks. The wood reached its destination, carried along by the current. This floating operation was the cheapest means of transportation and, ridding the wood of some of its metallic and earthy salts, increased its combustibility.

Following infiltration of water, the salinity ratio of the Meurthe river decreased to such an extent that in 1760 closure of the saltworks became inevitable. One immediate consequence, for want of outlets, was that the forests ceased to be exploited and the entire region was reduced to a state of dire poverty.

Faced with this tragic situation, the Bishop of Metz, Louis de Montmorency-Laval, had only two options open to him: abandon the forests or open a new wood-burning factory to use the fuel and provide work for an idle population. He chose the second solution, and decided to open a glass factory. This choice was all the more logical as Lorraine was traditionally a glassmaking area, producing both "large" glassware (window glass, mirrors, plate glass, etc.) and "small" glassware (bottles, tumblers, etc.). Besides, the real property of the Bishopric of Metz already included the Saint Quirin glass factory in the Moselle area. Setting up a wood-burning factory was subject to royal approval, and so Louis de Montmorency-Laval submitted his request to Louis XV, King of France, in the following terms:

"There is a lack of artistic glass-making in France, which is the reason why Bohemian products enter our country in such large quantities. Hence the phenomenal export of currency at a time when the Kingdom needs substantial sums of money to recover from the disastrous Seven-Years War." The argument was convincing and on October 16, 1764, at his Council held in Fontainebleau, the sovereign accepted the prelate's request.

The glass factory's location was decided on quickly. It would be Baccarat, or to be more precise, the land lying just across the Meurthe, on the right bank. The place seemed ideal: the village could provide the manpower necessary for the future industry. The river would enable wood from the surrounding forests to be floated, and the chosen site was suitable from the outset for possible large-scale operations.

Louis de Montmorency-Laval sought the help of a technician, Antoine Renaut, who came from Saint Quirin to manage the factory, and a financier, Léopold, Lord of Corny.

Each of the three associates owned a third of the

factory. In 1766, business started up with four furnaces and a workforce brought in by Antoine Renaut. Poor record-keeping accounts for the lack of information relating to the initial production, which was probably made up of "Bohemian-style" goblets in vogue during the period, window panes and mirrors.

In 1773, an unexpected event, the death of Leopold, Lord of Corny, led to the Company being dissolved. In order to repay the debts incurred by Leopold, Louis de Montmorency-Laval sold his share of the factory to Antoine Renaut, who also bought the deceased's shares from his heirs, thereby becoming the sole owner of the premises which he then called *Verrerie de Sainte-Anne* (Sainte Anne Glassworks), probably in honor of his mother.

Although the factory enjoyed genuine prosperity until 1789, it was not long before it suffered from the repercussions of the Revolution. The "freedom of labor" acknowledged by the Le Chapelier Law of June 14, 1791 led to an increase in the number of companies; in Lorraine, these were wood-burning factories whose installation brought about a sharp rise in the price of wood. When France declared war on the "King of Bohemia and Hungary," on April 20, 1792, the whole of Europe was in league against her. Borders were closed putting an end to all exports. The Sainte Anne Glassworks thus lost an important market. The requisitioning of raw materials, such as potash, exclusively reserved for making gun powder, combined with the departure of young men to war, first during the "levying" of 1793, then during the Empire Wars, with the introduction of conscription, progressively drove the factory to bankruptcy. In 1806, the three sons to whom Antoine Renaut

had given control of the Company four years earlier, were no longer able to settle their debts. On December 12 that same year, the factory was put up for auction. The buyer, Mr. Lippmann, a merchant from Verdun, attempted to keep it alive. To no avail. For the same reasons as his predecessors, Lippmann was unable to put the glassworks back on its feet. The factory struggled through until 1816, at which point its destiny changed radically.

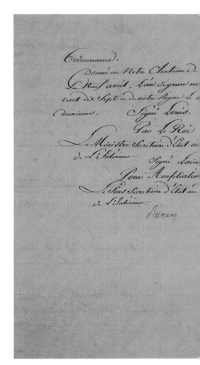

Edict of Louis XVIII

1817

D'Artigues:
The Vonêche Crystalworks
at Baccarat

1816 - 1822

Ordonnance du Roi.

With the end of the Napoleonic epic at Waterloo on June 18, 1815, the Empire was dismantled by the Second Treaty of Paris. The map of Europe was then redrawn.

The new configuration had a direct impact on the history of Baccarat. Belgium inherited the former French *département* of Sambre & Meuse where the Vonêche Crystalworks was located, in the Namur region. The owner, Aimé-Gabriel d'Artigues, was an eminent specialist in the crystal industry. Born in Paris in 1773, he was the adopted son of Jourdan, tenant from 1791 onwards of the Saint-Louis factory, the first in France to make lead crystal ten years earlier. After studying chemistry, d'Artigues held the position of director at Saint-Louis from 1791 to 1795. Seven years later, he bought the Vonêche Glassworks which he turned into a crystal factory in 1805. At the end of the first year, his efforts were rewarded by a silver medal bestowed on him by the Jury of the Exhibition of French Industrial Products.

Thus when Vonêche was declared not to be on French, but on Belgian territory, d'Artigues was faced with a two-fold problem. On the one hand, the very high customs duties along the new borders made it impossible for him to export his crystalware to France. On the other hand, the

Aimé-Gabriel d'Artigues

lifting of the Continental System imposed by Napoleon I, which deprived England of any trade with the continent opened up the European market to the many English crystal factories. Since this sudden competition threatened to be fatal to his company, d'Artigues obtained from the new French sovereign, Louis XVIII, the right to import his crystalware without paying duties for two years. This was on the proviso that it arrive in France in its raw state and be processed on site by means of cutting or engraving, and that he undertake to set up a crystal factory in the country at the same time.

On May 15, 1816, he bought up the Sainte Anne Glassworks, and on November 15 the same year, the *Etablissements de Vonêche's* first crystalware furnace was fired up.

Crystal was extremely popular at the time. It was part of the decorum of the new society born of the Revolution and the Empire. Under the Old Régime, drinking glasses were not permitted on the table but were brought by servants. After the Restoration, as befitting all "proper houses," table etiquette insisted on glasses being arranged on the table, each guest having at his disposal a water glass, two glasses for wine - one for red, the other one for white -, and a flute glass for champagne.

The appearance of gourmet restaurants such as Beauvilliers and Méot, opened before the Revolution, or the Café de Chartres, taken over by the famous Véfour in 1820, gave rise to a new *"art de vivre"*. Dinners and suppers were a pretext for genuine feasts for the palate, as well as the eyes.

The brilliance of crystal and the dancing light reflected in its engraved facets were an integral part of the splendor of dinner parties. The fashion of chandeliers made up of countless droplets of crystal, each one a prism of light playing with the candle flames, dates back to this period.

Baccarat's grand history started with d'Artigues. After seven years, however, his poor state of health and financial difficulties forced him to reduce his activities and part with his crystal factory.

On January 7, 1823, it was sold to three associates: Pierre-Antoine Godard-Desmarest, a Paris businessman, François-Marie-Augustin Lescuyer, a landowner, and Nicolas-Rémy Lolot, a merchant, both in Charleville.

Water set
1831

From the Restoration to the July Monarchy: the premises of fame

The main architect of this success, Pierre-Antoine Godard-Desmarest, was the first director of the corporation *"La Compagnie des Verreries et Cristalleries de Vonêche à Baccarat"*, a name it would keep until 1842.

Watchword: Perfection

Jean-Baptiste Toussaint was appointed manager of the factory, a position he already held in d'Artigues' time, and put in charge of running the establishment. As regards the workers, some of those who came from Belgium with d'Artigues had already trained local labor. The workforce comprised a hundred and fourteen glassmakers and a hundred and eleven engravers.

In 1823, at the National Exhibition of Industrial Products, Baccarat won its first gold medal. "The brilliance and delicacy of its crystal" was praised, crowning d'Artigues' achievements. However, it would be under the aegis of Pierre-Antoine Godard-Desmarest and his two associates that the crystalworks would compel recognition, first in France, then abroad. The three men took on a formidable task which would make Baccarat France's leading crystalworks within a few years. Pierre-Antoine Godard-Desmarest laid the foundations of Baccarat's structure, and it is thanks to him that the word "perfection" became the Company motto.

"Perfection" was based on the quality of the crystal and the laborforce.

The rigorous selection of raw materials guaranteed the quality of the crystal: sand came from Epernay, for it was purer than the local variety. Lead, purchased in Germany or England, was processed on site at the minium factory that d'Artigues had built close to the crystalworks in order to supervise its quality. Finally, most of the potash was imported from America as it contained minimum residues.

Louis XVIII

The Company was given its first prestigious order in 1823. While visiting the Exhibition of

Louis XVIII Stemware

1823

Industrial Products, King Louis XVIII noticed Baccarat's crystalware, which he praised for "its finish and esthetic qualities as well as for the low prices". A stemware pattern was then created for him. Samples of these, kept at the factory, formed the crystalworks' first archives of products.

Hot-work process

As for most French industries at the time, Baccarat's main concern was gaining a solid foothold in the French market. By offering a large range of perfectly made, mass-produced items at reasonable prices, the Company achieved this goal within a few years. A great many improvements were made in processing the pieces, particularly in molding techniques. However, the glassmaker's gestures would remain unchanged. The same movements still regulate life around the kilns, even today.

The crystal is *gathered* at a temperature of 1250°C with a metallic *blow-pipe* in a clay pot or *crucible* set in the furnace, openings pierced in the sides of the furnace provide access to the crucibles. The molten crystal sticks to the end of the blow-pipe which an assistant or *gamin* (boy) swiftly carries to the *place* where hot-work shaping takes place. The glassmaker takes hold of the blow-pipe turning it constantly in order to counterbalance the effect of gravity and spread the batch evenly as it cools down when in contact with the air. The liquid becomes pasty. Then the glassmaker starts blowing a bubble: the bowl takes shape. He rolls it on the marver, a smooth metal plate, while continuing to blow lightly to sketch the shape. This is done using rudimentary-looking tools: a wooden paddle, an extension of the glassmaker's free hand which defines and shapes the various masses, tongs with which to grab and elongate the crystal batch at the same time to produce the stem of the glass. Compasses are grabbed swiftly to check and adjust measurements, a pair of shears to cut the surplus crystal, called cullet, which will be used again in the melting of raw materials. Finally we come to the *pontil,* a solid metal rod at the end of which some molten crystal is picked off before being applied to the free end of the piece, enabling it to be removed from the blow-pipe. The piece is then transported, with the help of the *pontil,* to the annealing oven, where it is laid down on a sort of very slow conveyor-belt. It is left there to cool down gradually through decreasing temperature levels. This last step is essential as it reduces the internal stresses of the crystal which would otherwise burst at the slightest shock. All the glassmaker's operations are punctuated with goings back and forth between the workbench and the furnace to reheat the crystal which ceases to be malleable below 650°C. The first molded patterns are obtained at the glass-blowing stage by inserting the bottom of the bowl into the one-piece open molds which print

"Marabout" Water pitcher

circa **1833**

Dessert bowl
1835

Robinet pump
1824

the decorative motifs (large, vertical cuts either straight or in spirals, etc.)

A considerable improvement was made in 1824 thanks to the imagination of one of Baccarat's glassmakers, Ismaël Robinet: mold-blowing. A pump is used, the tip of which is fixed to the blow-pipe opening, to blow compressed air into the bowl, thereby replacing the glassmaker's breath, for certain pieces. The power of the compressed air meant that the shape of certain pieces could be molded and at the same time a motif imprinted on them.

This invention, which was immediately taken up by many glass and crystal factories, earned Robinet a gold medal from the Society for the Encouragement of French Industry and a stipend from Baccarat.

At the beginning of the 1830's, a new method called mold-pressing was used. Invented around 1827 in the United States by Enoch Robinson, it enabled the various engraved patterns to be imitated quite faithfully at a lower price.

The glassmaker's breath or piston's air was replaced by a solid metal core which drove the molten batch outwards to the sides of the mold while imprinting the pattern as it penetrated the

mold. This technique had the advantage of not leaving any traces inside the piece, as opposed to the first method in which each motif in relief has a counter hollow portion.

Due to the volume of the metal core, this type of molding only applied to objects which had an opening at least as wide as the bottom; it did not work with pieces narrower at the top than at the base, such as decanters. This technique of "solid molding" was applied to a large quantity of objects. It offered an unlimited range of motifs, from the simple "drapery" molding to a mixture of "diamonds" and "leaves," etc.

Cold-work process

After the annealing oven, the pieces are sent to the cutting workshop. Cutting has a decorative function, but is also used to eliminate imperfections such as the blow pipe mark, and to reinforce the effects of molding.

Pierre-Antoine Godard-Desmarest, who was concerned with modernizing the works, was granted permission by the Board of Directors assembled on October 6, 1824, to build a new cutting workshop on the Meurthe canal with a capacity for a hundred lathes, based on the English model, that is to say hydraulically powered, whereas up until that time they had been foot-driven by the cutters and engravers. Baccarat was the first crystal factory in France to adopt this system. The movement of the lathes drove a set of wheels or cutting stones which engraved the crystal following a pattern drawn on the piece with Judea bitumen. First the piece is placed against an iron wheel which bites into the crystal following the design. Sand and a thin trickle of water continuously poured on the crystal facilitate this first step. A second sandstone wheel, which also follows the motifs, removes the rough edges. The engravings are then softened using a wooden wheel and putty powder. Then comes the polishing phase, using a cork wheel which gives brilliance and transparency to the engravings. The polishing operation is then completed by using a cork wheel lined with wool.

All these operations are done freehand and demand infallible know-how on the part of the cutter. Again, as in the case of the glassmakers working around the furnaces, the engravers' methods have not changed since 1824.

First products

Molded pieces which were simple in shape during the early years were very successful. Unlike the engraved pieces, which were much more expensive, they were sold at the same price as plain pieces. It is thanks to them that crystal ceased to be a luxury item. It became part of the Bourgeois household: on the table, as stemware, fruit bowls, cheese covers, salt cellars, sugar bowls, mustard pots. Decorative objects, too, were inspired by the Greco-Roman Age: Medici vases, egg-shaped vases or jasmine vases, for example. Crystal also had a place in the bedroom with round bottles, Etruscan bottles, violet-holders and the "water suites" consisting of a water decanter, an orange blossom decanter, a stemmed glass, and a sugar bowl, all arranged on a crystal tray.

This variety of objects and their moderate prices accounted for Baccarat's initial success with the public.

Although this product range was bought by a new clientele, it in no way usurped the more luxurious engraved crystal, which was still much sought-after by buyers fond of its "rich" engravings. The Exhibition of 1827 gave

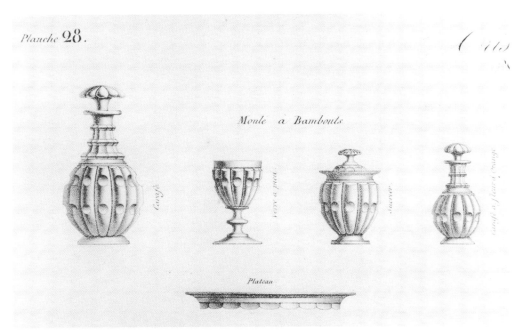

Planche **28**.

Moule à Bambouts

Plateau

Water set drawing
1831

Baccarat the opportunity to show its first prestigious achievements: two sumptuous Medici vases with deep, rich cuts which filled the public with awe. These pieces were made of clear crystal. Production of colored glass pieces, including opal crystal, was of little significance at the time. The colored pieces' relative lack of success at the 1827 Exhibition accounted for the fact that they were virtually abandoned in the early years.

Lighting fixtures

Baccarat's first lighting fixtures date back to 1824. Success was by no means immediate, due to foreign competition, mainly from Bohemia where prices were distinctively lower, and England whose reputation in this field went back to the end of the eighteenth century. The *Feuille hebdomadaire des Arts & Métiers* (Weekly Arts and Crafts Newsletter) dated Monday, August 27, 1827, gave an account of the Exhibition of French Industrial Products, stating with regard to Baccarat: "...The Company showed samples of new lighting fixtures which, by the perfection of the engraving and the vivid reflections, promise to free France from the tribute she is still paying to foreign countries for the composition of these beautiful chandeliers, which it behooves our bronze manufacturers to arrange in so elegant a manner."

Despite the lack of enthusiasm, Baccarat, French pioneer in this field, persisted in its endeavors. Within a few decades, it finally gained recognition. In the note addressed to the jury of the Exhibition of French Industrial Products in 1839, Pierre-Antoine Godard-Desmarest pointed out that "We are showing a collection of crystal for lighting fixtures for the third time. This is obviously not a novelty. Besides, we admit that these lighting fixtures are no more meticulous than our 1834 collection which did not leave much to be desired, but it is another attempt to try and convince lighting manufacturers to use our crystalware instead of the Bohemian variety, which is infinitely less refined than our own but favored because of its low price to which we hope never to stoop.

He concluded: "If this latest inducement remains fruitless, we shall have to give up these products all together ...."

However as the years passed, Baccarat acquired international renown for its chandeliers and other lighting fixtures, confirmed by the sumptuous orders for chandeliers from faraway palaces, as well as more modest orders from bourgeois households.

Competition

At the time, two companies were in competition with Baccarat. The first one, owned by the Chagot brothers, was the Montcenis crystal factory, in Creusot, previously called the *Manufacture de la Reine* (The Queen's workshop). It was founded in 1783 in Sèvres, in the enclosure of the Park of Saint Cloud. Based on the English model, using coal as fuel, it was transferred in 1787 close to the Creusot coal mines. Having been the first crystal factory during the Empire, it slowly collapsed under the Restoration.

Baccarat's most powerful competitor, however, was the Muntzthal-Saint Louis crystal factory. During the Restoration, the economic climate encouraged small factories to be set up, two of

Lustre n° 20813 à 36 bougies triple rose et vert, taille décor
Hauteur 1ᵐ60   Largeur 1ᵐ30.

Motif of a triple-cased chandelier

circa **1875**

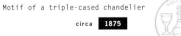

which located in the Paris area stood out: one in Choisy-Le-Roi, managed by the distinguished scholar, Georges Bontemps, the other in Bercy, founded by Jean-Alexandre Paris, well-known for his research into colored glass and for his enamelled incrustations in crystal.

Charles X

Within five years of its creation, from 1823 to 1828, the *Compagnie des Verreries et Cristalleries de Vonêche Baccarat* managed to gain a foothold in the French market.

In 1826, the Company purchased the Trélon glass factory located in the *département* of the North, with the aim of using it as an adjunct to the crystal factory to cover the needs of northern France. Unfortunately, Trélon would never achieve the output expected at the time of its purchase and would cause its parent company a good many problems. When its manager, Mr. Saint Pierre died in 1832, a victim of the cholera epidemic devastating Paris at the time, Jean-Baptiste Toussaint, dispatched to Trélon, found the factory in a terrible state. He decided to have a new furnace built. Trélon was then used as a subsidiary, in particular for making molded items. The factory would not be sold until 1874. Awarded two gold medals, first in 1823 then in 1827, Baccarat now enjoyed definite renown: the Company won acclaim on September 12, 1828 when King Charles X visited the crystal factory in spite of lashing rain, which was quite an event. Two large Medici vases decorated with sumptuous cuttings were given to him on this occasion. The Dauphin received a lavishly engraved ewer with the French coat of arms enameled on gold and inlaid in the crystal. His

mother, the Duchess of Angoulême, was presented with an eighteen-piece tea service. Following the visit, a service was made for the King.

However, the crisis of 1830 was looming. The "ultra" government formed by Prince Jules de Polignac in 1829 caused a split with Parliament. Despite the capture of Algiers by French troops on July 5, 1830, conflict seemed inevitable and finally broke out on July 25 with the promulgation of four royal enactments. One of these imposed censorship of the press. The riposte was immediate: barricades were erected in Paris at the instigation of typographers. The rebellion lasted three days and was nicknamed "The Three Glorious": July 28 to July 30. Charles X fled to England and the Duke of Orleans agreed to replace him on the throne. On August 9, Louis-Philippe, "the citizen-king", was proclaimed "King of the French People."

For Baccarat, as for many other industries, the July Revolution was a disaster. France then experienced a period of unrest with repercussions on the country's economic life. Stocks piled up at the crystal factory and in the warehouses, while the factory cut down production.

Louis-Philippe

Once the July Monarchy was in place, business picked up gradually. From 1830 to 1848, France underwent important changes. The country, now governed by the great liberal bourgeoisie, opened up to a phase of intense industrialization. Rural France, where transportation remained extremely slow, was gradually equipped with a railway network from 1837 onwards. The apparently unthreatened peace was favorable to a policy of economic investment.

Jean-Baptiste Toussaint

Charles X stemware

1828

"Three Glorious" tumbler

1831

Launay, Hautin & Cie (1832-1857)

Saint-Louis' director, François-Antoine Seiler, and Baccarat's director, Pierre-Antoine Godard-Desmarest, had been in contact with one another since 1829 with a potential marketing agreement in mind between the two companies. The agreement finally became a reality in 1830 with the joint decision to make a deal with the two main Paris wholesale merchants, Fresne Barbier and Jean-Baptiste Launay. A company taking effect as of January 1, 1832 for ten years and one month was registered in October 1831 under the corporate name of "Barbier, Launay & Cie". The head office was set up in Paris, at 30, rue de Paradis Poissonnière. The Choisy-le-Roi factory was allowed to join within a year, followed by its Bercy counterpart in 1833. After F. Barbier's death in 1832, the company changed its name to "Launay, Hautin & Cie." Its aim was to smother competition and guarantee its own outlets. Joint illustrated price lists were published regularly (the origins of certain pieces were specified). The first crystal factory to suffer from this

association was Montcenis where the furnaces were turned off in 1828, not to be fired up again until October 1831. The owners of the establishment, the Chagot brothers, wanted to be admitted into the company but neither Baccarat nor Saint-Louis was willing to accept such an important partner. The only solution to eliminate this potential competition was to buy up the factory. After a visit to the premises, Pierre-Antoine Godard-Desmarest and François-Antoine Seiler agreed to purchase it. As soon as the contract of sale was signed on July 9, 1832, the crystal factory was closed. The molds and any useful equipment were divided up between Baccarat and Saint-Louis. The buildings and lands would be sold four years later to the Schneider brothers, who owned the Creusot ironworks, marking the end of the former *Manufacture de la Reine*. The Launay, Hautin & Cie Company was finally disbanded in 1857. The headquarters in Paris were divided up between Baccarat and Saint-Louis where the two still remain today.

New processes, new products

The 1834 Exhibition of French Industrial Products once again awarded Baccarat's products a gold medal. Despite the appearance in France of numerous glass factories producing the same type of molded objects as the crystalworks at lower cost, the real danger came from Bohemia. France, having given in to the fashion for colorless or opaline glass and crystal, more or less forgot coloring methods, which is the exact opposite of what happened in Bohemian glassworks, where these techniques were improved considerably. Soon, their mastery of

Launay, Hautin & Cie catalogue
circa 1833

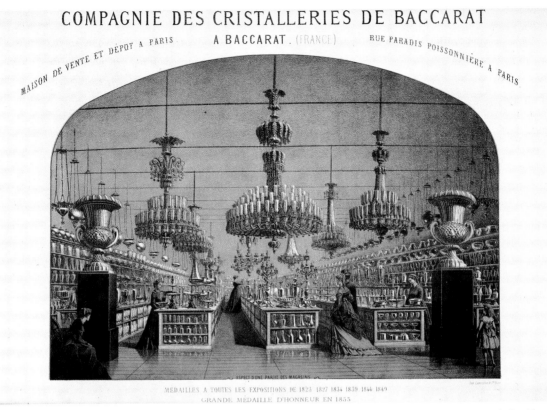

COMPAGNIE DES CRISTALLERIES DE BACCARAT
A BACCARAT. (FRANCE)
MAISON DE VENTE ET DÉPOT A PARIS.
RUE PARADIS POISSONNIÈRE A PARIS.

MÉDAILLES A TOUTES LES EXPOSITIONS DE 1823 1827 1834 1839 1844 1849
GRANDE MÉDAILLE D'HONNEUR EN 1855

Baccarat showroom rue de Paradis, Paris

circa **1860**

various coloring techniques, such as densely opaque jet-black or red glass called hyalith glass or lithyalin glass, an opaque marbled glass in imitation of semi-precious stones, enabled them to recapture the international market. Despite import restrictions in France, colored glassware was smuggled in, and from 1835 onwards, received widespread interest. The reaction in France was immediate: glass industrialists rushed to Bohemia in search of the secret production techniques which they managed to bring back. In addition, in 1836, the Society for the Promotion of French Industry launched a series of contests to imitate the Bohemian pieces and eliminate threatening competition.

In 1838, Baccarat dispatched its future managing director, Emile Godard-Desmarest, and its manager, Jean-Baptiste Toussaint, to Bohemia. Upon their return, the results were felt immediately: Baccarat started producing colored crystal, either colored throughout the mass or encased by superimposing two layers of crystal. The richness and extensive variety of shades offered earned the company another gold medal on the occasion of the 1839 Exhibition of French Industrial Products. As Mr. Dumas, the reporter for the glass section of the exhibition stated: "Up until now, Bohemia ...(also) produced colored goblets in vivid, bright, rich and varied tones much admired by glass lovers. This exhibition has proved that we no longer have anything to learn from Bohemia."

The "classic" decorations and shapes in vogue during the first years were followed by another fashion, inspired by borrowings from the Middle Ages, the Renaissance, and a degree of exoticism from China and Japan. The number of molds was then increased by using combinations of these.

During their stay in Bohemia, Emile Godard-Desmarest and Jean-Baptiste Toussaint had managed to "steal away" a glassmaker and an engraver. After countless difficulties, the artisans arrived in Baccarat in 1839. At the time, the crystal factory employed 900 workers, including 208 glassmakers, some 400 cutters, three engravers and eight gilders.

This highly qualified workforce mastered the full range of manufacturing and decorating techniques.

The note sent by Baccarat for the 1839 Exhibition specified that two-thirds of production was sold in France, the rest going mainly to the different American states, as well as various countries bordering France.

Thus Pierre-Antoine Godard-Desmarest had reached the objective he had set for himself in 1823. In 1839, the moment had come for him to give the reins to his son Emile.

Although the first ten years of the July Monarchy were a prosperous period, the overall climate quickly deteriorated after 1840, France being hit headlong by the economic crises of 1837 in England and the United States. Production slowed down to such an extent that one of the three furnaces had to be turned off.

At this stage, François-Eugène de Fontenay arrived at Baccarat, a man whose work would turn the crystal factory into a model of modernity.

François-Eugène de Fontenay (1810-1884)

In 1829, François-Eugène de Fontenay registered at the recently founded Ecole Centrale des Arts et Manufactures. He left the school three years later to run the Plaine-de-Walsch glassworks, owned by the Baron de Klinglin, in the Meurthe area. Under his guidance, this small traditional factory gained in the space of a few short years a remarkable reputation for both its modern operations and the innovative nature of its products. Such dazzling progress earned the factory a gold medal at the Exhibition of Industrial Products in Nancy, in which it took part for the first time in 1838.

The first research conducted by François-Eugène de Fontenay at Plaine-de-Walsch covered glass coloring processes. In 1839, he won three of the contests organized by the Society for the Promotion of French Industry, two of which were directly related to the coloring process. One concerned the process of enamelling with vitrifiable colors painted on glass and fixed in an annealing oven. He shared the award with Jean-François Robert, painter-decorator at the Royal Manufacture of Sèvres, with whom de Fontenay had perfected this decorating technique, from which the Plaine-de-Walsch factory was the first to benefit in 1836. Jean-François Robert then adapted the results obtained with glass for use on crystal.

The second prize awarded to François-Eugène de Fontenay and Georges Bontemps, manager of the Choisy-le-Roi glassworks, honored their respective work on the casing or overlay method. The method consists of covering a first layer of usually clear glass or crystal during the blowing stage with a second layer of colored crystal. The outer layer is cut away, allowing the inner clear layer to appear, producing a double coloring effect. Later on, other layers of glass or crystal were added, further enhancing the coloring effect by cutting.

François-Eugène de Fontenay traveled to Germany many times to discover new techniques which could be used at the Plaine-de-Walsch factory. In 1837, he brought back an engraver with him called Günther. Günther later opened an engraving school and one of his students, Jean-Baptiste Simon would follow François-Eugène de Fontenay to Baccarat. His research also led him to improve the working of furnaces, in particular using a process consisting of increasing combustion by directing an air draft onto the flame inside the furnace, the wood used to feed the furnace being perfectly dried and stacked. This process meant that the fusion process could be controlled, enabling the glassmakers' working hours to be regulated. Up until then, they could be summoned by a bell at any time of the day or night, according to the "whims" of the fusion process. This explains why glassmakers' lodgings were traditionally just a stone's throw away from the *halle,* where the furnaces were located.

When, at the end of 1840, as a result of differences, François-Eugène de Fontenay left Plaine-de-Walsch and the Vallerysthal glassworks owned by the Baron de Klinglin since 1838, Baccarat immediately hired him to assist Jean-Baptiste Toussaint. The factory enjoyed forthwith all the improvements to the furnaces, coloring processes and decolorization techniques perfected by François-Eugène de Fontenay at Plaine-de-Walsch.

On the perfection of clear crystal

One of the main difficulties in making clear

Wine decanter

1835

Glassmakers at work

François-Eugène de Fontenay

crystal is obtaining a perfectly transparent material, free from any trace of coloring. Despite efforts to purify raw materials, some metal oxides always remain, a minute quantity of which is enough to give a slight coloring to the crystal. These oxides are also present in the clay contained in the crucibles and found on the glassmakers' tools. To overcome this problem, it was customary to incorporate manganese oxide into the initial compound in order to counterbalance the effects of metal oxides. Even so, the results still left much to be desired. Upon his arrival in Baccarat, François-Eugène de Fontenay strove to solve this problem. He finally succeeded by replacing the manganese oxide with nickel oxide. The decolorization process was a considerable leap forward for the crystal industry, and Baccarat was once again awarded a gold medal at the Exhibition of French Industrial Products in 1844.

From the colors of crystal to agate glass

When Pierre-Antoine Godard-Desmarest and his associates took over the Crystalworks in 1823, the only "fantasy" pieces were made of opal crystal, so called because of its resemblance to the stone. This type of crystal is distinguished by its milky white aspect, with varying degrees of opaqueness, and a slightly orangy transparency. It is produced using a process already known at the time of the Venetians which consists of adding lime phosphate obtained from charred and crushed bones to the raw materials. A reaction takes place when the compound is taken out of the crucible: the crystal, transparent at the time of gathering, becomes opaque during the shaping process. The more the vessel is processed and the greater the number of warming and cooling phases, the more opaque the piece

becomes. It is therefore a question of measuring out the proportion of lime phosphate in relation to the length of the glassmaker's operation and the final effect desired.

Baccarat's archives do not include any objects in opal crystal dating from this period. However, the catalog of the Museum of Sèvres, published in 1845, mentions a milky white goblet displayed at the 1823 Exhibition, donated by Pierre-Antoine Godard-Desmarest.

Production of opal crystal remained minor, mainly reproducing objects usually made of china, such as the plates, salad bowls and strawberry bowls presented in 1827.

The same is true of colored crystal items, whether they be opal or not. There again, until 1838, these products remained secondary. According to the note written by Pierre-Antoine Godard-Desmarest about the 1839 Exhibition, it seems that the Company was somehow reluctant to "enter the field of fashion, and we should add the most whimsical sort of fashion, with no established rules, given that no utilitarian considerations are involved. Decorating a shelf, a chest of drawers, a lady's dressing table, such is, to a greater or lesser degree, the only purpose served by these products."

"Pâte de riz" creamer (agate glass)
circa 1849

Harcourt Stemware

1841

Chimney bottle with sky-blue agate glass decoration

circa **1844**

In 1840, the fad for colored crystals, whether colored in the mass or by superimposed layers, was at its peak. The progress achieved in the field of chemistry brought about a scientific rather than empirical approach to handling glass coloring agents: salts or metal oxides. It was thanks to François-Eugène de Fontenay that Baccarat soon excelled in this new field, which from 1842 onwards also expanded to include a new variety of glass, lead-free and particularly rich in silica.

This glass, produced after the fashion of Bohemian glassworks, was very bright and non-reflective. It had a milky and translucent appearance and was extremely smooth and soft to the touch. Referred to as "agate glass" by Baccarat, when white it was also described by the generic terms of "pâte de riz" or "alabaster glass". Its particularly refined composition, without agents which made it opaque, underwent an extremely delicate fusion process during which a multitude of microscopic gas bubbles developed in the batch. As a matter of fact, the agate glass' mark of authenticity lay in the presence of small grains showing through the light, visible to the naked eye. Badly performed fusion produced either a totally clear glass or a glass inside which conglomerates appeared, referred to in glassmakers' jargon as "stones". This form of production was to become one of Baccarat's successful innovations.

With the creation of an extremely varied palette of colors, competition from Bohemia would be permanently overshadowed.

The famous "sky-blue," very often used by Baccarat, was obtained in 1842 by adding copper oxide, whereas cobalt oxide gave ultramarine blue.

The pink obtained by precipitating gold salts mixed with tin (flash ruby) appeared in 1847, overlaid on white agate glass. As gold salts were very expensive, they were only used in very thin cased layers.

Various tones of green were also invented at the time, including emerald green, with iron oxides, or pale green produced by copper oxide on opal crystal.

The color palette appeared to be limitless. For twenty years, all sorts of shades were obtained by varying the proportions of the various oxides and mixing them together.

While he was still at Plaine-de-Walsch, François-Eugène de Fontenay had taken an interest in the coloring powers of uranium oxide. This oxide, already used by Bohemian glassmakers, has the peculiarity, when mixed with clear agate glass, of producing a dichromatic effect characterized by a yellow aspect in refraction and a green aspect in reflection.

In 1842, François-Eugène de Fontenay created the famous "chrysoprase" or parrot green by mixing uranium oxide and copper oxide. Widely used, this green shade appeared in many decorations. The same compound, in different proportions, produced "imperial green", in 1861. These uranium oxide-based colorings were used exclusively on agate glass, since the lead contained in crystal reacted against the fluorescent and luminous properties of uranium. In the twentieth century, uranium oxide would be replaced by vanadium oxide. Unlike crystal, agate glass cannot be engraved. Further, it had the disadvantage of hardening extremely quickly as soon as it comes out of the furnace. So it had to be worked using molds.

On the occasion of the 1849 Exhibition of

Chimney bottle in dichromatic glass

circa **1844**

Agate glass vase

1849

French Industrial Products, Baccarat displayed a wide range of objects in agate glass, decorated with highly astounding molded elements: masks borrowed from mythology (heads of fauns and Bacchus), elaborate handles "enabling shapes to be varied, which had otherwise been so monotonous beforehand and so unartistic," as underscored in the jury's report. The jury once again awarded the Baccarat Company a gold medal. This period also saw the remarkable production of opal crystal objects painted with polychrome and gilded enamels, using the technique jointly perfected in 1836 by François-Eugène de Fontenay and Jean-François Robert which had earned them a prize from the Society for the Encouragement of French Industry in 1839. The art reached its peak with the magnificent floral ornaments executed in Paris by the same Jean-François Robert between 1843 and 1855 for Launay, Hautin & Cie, then went into slow decline. The production of agate glass and opalized crystal continued successfully until the last quarter of the nineteenth century at which point fashions changed and it was finally abandoned. It was not until the beginning of the twentieth century that, resurrected from the past to satisfy a new market, i.e., antique dealers, that agate glass and opal crystal, henceforth called "opaline," found a new clientele among collectors. The same fate was shared by another type of product: paperweights, *millefiori* and sulphides, whose golden age was between 1845 and 1860, were also rediscovered in the twentieth century thanks to collectors.

Millefiori

Other countries began to organize exhibitions to show their products, similar to the Exhibition of

"Church" paperweight

1853

French Industrial Products. They attracted as many potential customers as industrialists from abroad. In 1845, the Paris Chamber of Commerce dispatched Eugène Péligot, a professor at the Royal Conservatory of Arts and Crafts, to Vienna where Austria was exhibiting its own industrial production. Eugène Péligot went with Jean-Baptiste Toussaint and two managers from the Saint-Louis glassworks. After his visit, he wrote a report published in 1846, in which he emphasized the presentation by the Venetian glassmaker, Pietro Bigaglia. His exhibits included "... *mille fiori*, round paperweights of clear glass containing tightly packed little tubes of all shapes and colors, assembled in order to produce the effect of an array of flowers."

From 1845 onwards, Baccarat and Saint-Louis strove to produce these spheres full of charm and poetry which required a particularly delicate technique. The "subject" at the heart of the millefiori is composed by putting together a large number of little crystal canes. They are made by dipping a blowpipe in a pot of molten crystal; the batch thus gathered is embedded in a second layer of crystal of a different color, then a third. Once this operation is completed, a second blowpipe is attached to the free end of the batch and the crystal stretched over several meters so that the diameter of the formed "thread" or strip only measures a few millimeters. Once cooled, the crystal rod is cut with a "straw cutter" into several slices or "canes" ready to be used. Transversely, in the middle, they show the first color gathered, surrounded by the second, etc. The canes are often combined; laid in the bottom of a pot, they are covered with a clear molten crystal matrix and put through the same stretching process in order to form new rods.

By putting the crystal gathered at the beginning of the process in a mold with a motif either on its sides, or hollow at the bottom, when it is removed from the mold, the crystal is imprinted with these motifs. It is then immediately dipped into a pot filled with crystal of a different color to coat it. Stretched, then cooled, it forms a new rod which once sliced shows the initial motif.

The paperweight production process can then begin. The canes are laid vertically on a metal disk according to a defined motif, mixing rods of different colors and shapes - circles, stars, arrows, human or animal silhouettes, letters (B for Baccarat), or numbers indicating the date of manufacture, etc. Once these elements have been gathered together, the disk is heated and covered with a layer of molten crystal, using a blowpipe. By welding the canes together, the crystal enables them to be removed from their support. The assembly is then marvered smooth before being coated with a new layer of crystal. The piece's round shape is obtained using a hot-working process in the hollow of a wooden instrument known as a *forming block*.

Another technique is also used to make paperweights, their decorative patterns being fashioned using a blowlamp. To produce isolated flowers, flat or standing bouquets, fruit, vegetables, butterflies, and reptiles, the glassmaker gathers little slices of canes of various colors which he then models using the blowlamp flame, small pincers and shears, to give them shapes for assembly: flower petals, butterfly wings, snake scales, etc. The completed pattern is laid on a mold to be encased in a crystal batch also fashioned with a forming block. The famous standing bouquet which gives a three-dimensional view of the bouquet, is modeled in a different way. Once all the elements of the bouquet have been assembled, they are placed "upside down" in a convex-shaped mold in which molten crystal is poured, enveloping the base of the future piece which can be turned over using a pontil. The other side or top of the paperweight is then covered with crystal before being rounded with the forming block.

Once the hot-work process is over, the pieces are sent to the cold-work workshops to be handled by the engravers, who either simply cut a star in the bottom of the ball or, more elaborately, engrave facets on the sides.

If the sphere is encased in several layers of crystal, the engraver intervenes between applications, leaving windows or "pontils" through which, once the piece has been polished, both the various layers of colors and the elaborate motif decorating its core appear. Such pieces are called "overlay."

Millefiori were extremely popular between 1845 and 1860. During this so-called "classic" period, three crystalworks had the privilege of producing the most beautiful creations: Baccarat, Saint-Louis and Clichy (established in 1838). Each of them had its own specific character which distinguished it from the other two. Among Baccarat's creations, one deserves particular attention. One day in 1848, Jean-Baptiste Toussaint came across a series of paper cut-outs done by his nine-year old nephew, Joseph-Emile Gridel, of animal figures sketched in a fashion both naive and realistic. These small subjects (roosters, deer, dogs, goats, etc.) captured Jean-Baptiste Toussaint's imagination to such an extent that he had them reproduced in molds for use in making canes for paperweights.

Some patterns are in themselves signatures of

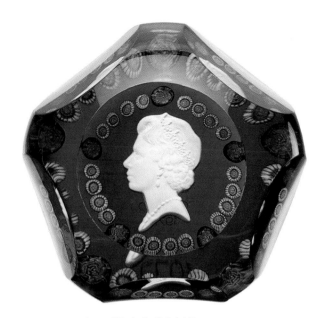

Queen Elizabeth II Sulphide

1953

Paperweight 19th century

Baccarat: the pansy, a symbolic flower of this period of triumphant romanticism, unsettling snakes on a rocky background, ephemeral butterflies caught in full flight in the crystal mass, and so on. In 1848, during the Revolution preceding the accession to power by the *Prince-President*, Louis Napoleon, Emperor-to-be, glass-makers used the three colors of the French flag to compose flower arrangements. Lastly, it is worth noting that the first signed and dated pieces produced by Baccarat were paperweights bearing the initial B for Baccarat and the year of manu-facture, by means of strips inserted into the crystal.

Sulphides

The term refers to crystal spheres enclosing a cameo. They were fashionable before the *millefiori*. The time-honored technique for producing sulphides, also called "cameo incrustations," was rediscovered in Bohemia during the second half of the eighteenth century. A few years later, around 1790, research was conducted in France by Henri-Germain Boileau who came up with a mixture of kaolin and potash silicate, which he used to produce the first incrustations. They

Drawings by Joseph-Emile Gridel

were molded in relief, fired and encased in molten glass. At the beginning of the nineteenth century, in England, the success of biscuit medallions produced by the Wedgwood company encouraged glassmaker Apsley Pellatt (1791-1863) to file a patent of invention for a similar kaolin and potash-silicate-based paste: *cristallo-ceramie.* The composition of cristallo-ceramie meant that it could withstand the high temperatures of molten crystal. At the beginning of the Restoration, this technique was brought back to France from England by a survivor of the 1789 Revolution, Pierre-Honoré Boudon de Saint-Amans (1774-1858), who worked closely with the Montcenis crystal factory, the first in France to develop this type of production.

Later on, Baccarat successfully took up production with sulphides of religious subjects or motifs celebrating well-known historical figures: Joan of Arc, the Kings of France, Napoleon the First and Josephine, Napoleon the Third, British royalty in the form of Queen Victoria and Prince Albert, etc. The glass spheres were remarkable for the quality of their finish and the richness of the colored backgrounds from which the little white figurines stood out.

Sulphides and millefiori were not only used in spheres but also on objects: scent bottles, decanters, vases, banister balls, goblets are just some examples. In the nineteenth century, these spheres had only shortlived success. Forgotten at the end of the Second Empire, they owed their revival to enthusiasts who succumbed to their indefinable charm at the beginning of the twentieth century and put together prestigious collections. As a result of legacies and donations, they found their way into museums. Since then, a great many works have been written about them.

In the twentieth century, the "revival" of these series was linked to a rather moving episode. When the first church was built in Baccarat in 1853, a glassmaker called Martin Kayzer produced a millefiori paperweight which he included in the foundations of the building. In 1945, the church collapsed as a result of Allied bombing. During its reconstruction in 1951, the paperweight was discovered in the rubble. This find gave the crystal factory the opportunity to rekindle the magic of these antique creations. An artist, Gilbert Poillerat (1902-1989) gave a modern character to the traditional objects by relaunching the making of commemorative sulphides on the occasion of the coronation of Elizabeth the Second, Queen of England. Baccarat also owes him a range of paperweights inspired by the signs of the zodiac. Since then, millefiori and sulphides have been produced every year in limited editions to the good fortune of numerous professional or amateur collectors in love with these beguiling crystal objects.

Baccarat during the 1848 unrest

All the improvements brought about by François-Eugène de Fontenay enabled Baccarat to offer a wide range of reasonably priced quality objects, which made the Company the leading crystalworks. The competition that sustained the rivalry with Saint-Louis was tempered by their joint trading company, Launay, Hautin & Cie. Among the establishments founded in the wave of prosperity under the July Monarchy, the Clichy glassworks, set up in 1838 by Rouyer and Maës, was the only one able to compete with the two major companies without threatening them in any way.

In 1842, the life of the *Compagnie des Verreries et Cristalleries de Vonêche Baccarat* was extended by royal order to December 31, 1882, under the name *Compagnie des Verreries et Cristalleries de Baccarat*. Until 1847, its shareholders were able to rejoice over the company's annual reports. However, the serious agricultural crisis which had plagued Europe since 1846 reached France in 1847. On February 22, 1848, revolution broke out in Paris. Two days later, King Louis-Philippe was forced to abdicate paving the way for the Republic which would be led a few months later by the *Prince-President*, Louis Napoleon Bonaparte, who became Napoleon the Third. At the start of the Revolution, most of Baccarat's orders were cancelled, and for two years, the factory worked only erratically. During this difficult time, the Company's main concern was to keep its workforce in place. This was the only way that Baccarat could wait for better days. Its directors' wisdom and Jean-Baptiste Toussaint's and François-Eugène de Fontenay's knowledge were worth little without the incomparable know-how of the staff who had been through long years of training in the workshops. Their leaving Baccarat would mean the end of the Company. A system of compensation was thus introduced for days when there was no work. The crisis hit the Choisy-le-Roi crystalworks mercilessly, and it was forced to close in 1847. A year later, Bercy gave up all crystal production and concentrated on ordinary glass. This left Baccarat and Saint-Louis alone with the Launay, Hautin & Cie Company. France finally managed to overcome the crisis, albeit gradually. The railway network was also expanding, and in 1849, the Paris-Strasbourg line was inaugurated. From that time on, Baccarat's delivery times to

the Paris warehouse at 30 rue Paradis-Poissonnière were cut to three days from the previous ten. That same year, François-Eugène de Fontenay took over the running of the factory from Jean-Baptiste Toussaint who was appointed managing director. Two years later, spurred on by the free trade spirit, England organized the first Great Exhibition. Prince Albert's message -"Artistic and industrial creations are not the privilege of one nation; they belong to the entire world" - fell on deaf ears in France, and many of the nation's industrialists, including Baccarat and Saint-Louis, refused to go to the Crystal Palace, the cast iron and glass monument built for the occasion in London. The reasons for their refusal were manifold and could be attributed to a degree of fear in the face of potential competition coupled with fierce opposition to any idea of free trade. After much hesitation, Clichy, the sole representative of the French crystal industry, agreed to go. In his report written after the exhibition, Eugène Péligot deplored Baccarat's absence, pointing out that the company "has become a model of its kind, both for the perfection and variety of the products leaving the factory and the well-being the company has bestowed on its many employees." The report mentioned the existence of some ten crystalworks in France, the most important of them being Baccarat, with production estimated at two million francs a year followed by Saint-Louis (one million eight hundred thousand francs), then Clichy (seven hundred thousand), etc. Baccarat and Saint Louis were the only ones working with wood as opposed to coal. The report also seems to indicate that the cost of raw materials was exceedingly high in France in comparison with England, Bohemia and Belgium.

Bowl in "pâte de riz" and "chrysoprase" Decoration painted in gold

1855

From fame
to supremacy : the splendor
of the Second Empire

1848 - 1870

Louis Napoleon Bonaparte, elected President for four years in 1848, instigated a coup d'état to keep power in his hands, on December 2, 1851, the anniversary of the coronation of his uncle Napoleon the First and his victory at Austerlitz. He managed to hold on to power not just for the four years as stipulated by the 1848 Constitution, but for ten. Bolstered by his success, a year later he proclaimed himself Emperor after a triumphant plebiscite.

1855-1867: from one World's Fair to the Next

The establishment of the Second Empire in France would be the starting point for a period of economic growth accompanied by a remarkable industrial boom, as testified the Paris World's Fair of 1855. This first exhibition was dedicated to the power of the steam engine; it included a huge gallery where a multitude of machines operated round the clock producing deafening noises before the eyes of a flabbergasted public. In the face of such gigantic scale, Baccarat presented, among the thousand objects it exhibited, two huge candelabras over five meters high each holding a bouquet of 90 candles spread

Opal glass vase, decoration painted in gold and enamel

1855

across its one-meter-eighty diameter and a chandelier with 140 lights almost five meters high and three meters wide. It was the first time that such imposing pieces had ever been produced in France. A British firm from Birmingham owned by a Mr. Osler was the only one to also exhibite a candelabra comparable to Baccarat's. In his *Note on the glassworks and ceramics of the Paris Great Exhibition* published in 1857 in the Society of Civil Engineers' Report, Mr. Salvetat pointed out that "the lighting, as displayed by Baccarat's candelabras and chandeliers, has reached the level of an art form in itself: they are no longer ill-thought-out arrangements of crystal pieces cut unmethodically; everything is calculated in order to break up the light and obtain the greatest brilliance. These pieces are the greatest expression of the powerful means at Baccarat's disposal ...."

A large bowl and two vases in white agate glass decorated with chrysoprase agate patterns, each one meter eighty-five high, also drew a lot of attention. The elegant shapes, exceptional quality of the crystal and the diversity of the products exhibited received unanimous praise and earned Baccarat the medal of honor. The note submitted by the crystalworks on the occasion of the Exhibition mentioned one hundred and twenty five workers' families living on the premises. A mutual aid fund for the cutters, partly financed by the Company, had been in operation for twenty years to help widows, orphans and the sick. The cutters had also enjoyed a pension fund since 1851. In the event of sickness or unemployment, the glassmakers working at the furnaces were paid their full salary or two thirds of it. In addition, they drew a pension granted by the Company upon retirement. Workers' children were also given free primary education. 1855 was a particularly prosperous year for France. The Crimean War declared jointly by France and England in 1854 against the Tsar of Russia ended in victory for the two Allies in

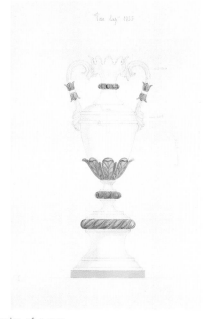

Drawing of a vase
1855

1856. The French task force was under the command of Marshal Canrobert who honored the Baccarat crystalworks with a visit.

The end of an era was marked for Baccarat when its trading partnership with Saint-Louis was discontinued in 1857, and on the death of its managing director, Jean-Baptiste Toussaint, in 1858. The vacant position was taken up for the second time by Emile Godard-Desmarest who would occupy it until 1867.

The Emperor initiated a policy of major works, notably the restructuring of Paris undertaken by the Prefect of the Seine, Baron Georges Eugène Haussmann with the Emperor's "assistance." Unsalubrious blocks were destroyed, monuments cleared, and large thoroughfares opened up, crisscrossing the capital from east to west and north to south. A sewer system was also built. The

Stemware

1858

city's development, with the construction of buildings, private mansions, such as those erected around Monceau Park, brought Baccarat a new clientele. The Bourgeoisie grew considerably richer, banks were created, and money circulated encouraging investment.

However, new concerns seemed bound to cast a shadow over the future. Napoleon the Third secretly negotiated a free trade treaty with England, which was finally signed on January 23, 1860. The first consequence of this "customs' coup d'etat" was a sharp fall in import duties. Until that time protectionism had guaranteed industrialists their prerogatives on the French market. Most were fiercely opposed to the treaty and had to change their pricing policy for fear of fighting the competition on unequal terms particularly since a similar treaty was signed

with Prussia in 1862.

Beginning in 1860 Baccarat reacted to the situation by consolidating its foreign markets. Increasing the number of sales outlets abroad, whether it be in Europe, the Orient or on the American continent, had the advantage of compensating for potential losses in the wake of unexpected events in one or other of the crystalworks' "client countries". In 1861 with the outbreak of the American Civil War, Baccarat lost an important market. The repercussions were felt straight away: the workshops slowed down production and stocks piled up. This was not too disastrous, however, and the situation was brought under control as of 1863 partly due to an appreciable increase in exports.

The Emperor's Minister of Trade, Eugène Rouher, invited Baccarat to take part in the third

World's Fair, which was once again to be held in London, as in 1851. Again, Baccarat declined the offer, less out of fear of competition than in defiance of a governement which had dared to repeal protectionism. The other reason for this refusal was more implicit: the expenses incurred for taking part in this kind of event were extremely high when set against the potential business which the company stood to gain. Once again, the directors' wisdom prevailed over a desire to exhibit. At the time, Baccarat was more concerned with technical improvements to the factory.

Siemens Furnace

In 1862, an outstanding technological advance transformed the crystalworks right to its very core. Since its creation, few changes had taken place in the furnaces' operation, apart from improvements made by François-Eugène de Fontenay. One of the Company's main concerns after 1823 was the prohibitive price of wood. Nevertheless, Siemens, a German engineer living in England, invented a furnace fired not directly by the flames but by the combustion gas from the wood. Baccarat bought the exclusive rights to use this system in France. As stated in the 1861-1862 annual report, this saved a considerable amount of money: "a 31% saving was achieved over wood-fired furnaces ... The glass melted by using gas, when it was successfully produced, was clearer and shinier than that produced in wood-fired kilns." The use of these furnaces allowed the Company to lower its prices and combat competition effectively. In point of fact, the opening up of borders to imports had little influence on Baccarat's domestic market. Its

prices and renown had earned the Company a constantly growing clientele. At the same time, progress in the field of engraving would also bring about change.

From wheel-engraving to acid-etched engraving: the Kessler process

Since 1839, wheel-engraving had developed and improved consistently on account of engravers' skill backed up by years and years of experience. It entails the use of small copper wheels of different thicknesses which bite into the crystal following a pattern, leaving in their wake a hollow mat imprint. While working, the engraver constantly applies a small pad coated with a mixture of an abrasive substance (emery or diamond powder) and turpentine to the sharp edge of the wheel, which enables the crystal to be engraved "smoothly." The motifs are then polished with a lead-wheel. As with gilding, this cold-working decoration process is particularly prized. Whether applied alone or combined with cutting, the engraving process is appealing because of the airiness of the patterns obtained, mixing patterns of little flowers, acanthus leaves and wreaths and leaves with geometric designs, from the single line underlining the rim of the glass to diamonds, crosses, olives, etc.
In the light of the increasing success of wheel-engraved pieces, Baccarat endeavored to find a way of increasing production and lowering prices, as they were actually very expensive. The price was set to take account of the highly qualified staff required and the amount of time taken, which varied according to the complexity of the patterns. Since the seventeenth century, various experiments had been carried out in

Europe, especially in Nuremberg, on the effects of different acids on glass. However, it was only during the second half of the nineteenth century that industrial use of acid was made possible thanks to the work of chemist L. Kessler. In 1855, he initially managed to produce a sufficient quantity of hydrofluoric acid to market it. The recent invention of gutta-percha, a latex-based material with high insulating properties, enabled it to be transported and stored with minimum risk on account of its double wrapping. The container of acid was itself encased in another. Some ten years later in 1864, L. Kessler perfected an acid bath engraving method. The technique consists in coating the piece to be engraved with a mixture of wax and turpentine applied under heat. The motif of the intended engraving is traced on the piece with a point. Then the piece is immersed in acid, for varying lengths of time depending on the depth of the desired engraving. Baccarat bought the process and put it into practice immediately. Acid-engraving did not however replace the wheel process. It simply allowed the Company to attract a clientele who could not afford genuine hand-cut jewels. On the subject of engravers, the testimony left by Turgan, the director of the *Moniteur Universel*, in his book published in 1863, Les grandes usines (Large factories), is impressive in the degree of maturity that this art attained at Baccarat: "Some engravers are so skilled that on a rather thick glass, they can carve hollow bas reliefs which, with the light shining through, produce the effect of real sculptures. We have seen a beautiful portrait of Mr. Godard-Desmarest's father by Mr. Simon. The same engraver showed us a plaque depicting colored flowers whose nuances were obtained by etching

Water goblet

circa **1863**

at different depths into a sheet made of several superimposed layers of colored crystal." Jean-Baptiste Simon's genius would be revealed to the general public, at the 1867 World's Fair.

Crucibles

In his account, Turgan devoted considerable space to refractory pot and crucible making. These parts are made of refractory clays mixed with cimente from old broken crucibles. The mixture is kneaded mechanically then "stamped out." It is stored in a cellar for a "rest" period after which it is brought back up to be fashioned in the pottery workshop. Produced in the form of wads arranged in a wooden mold, the crucible is then gradually heated in a drying oven. Before taking its place in the *halle*, it remains a whole day in a special oven to be white-heated. All these operations are performed with great care. The crucible has to be reliable, in other words,

contain as few impurities as possible and be
perfectly heatresistant.

Baccarat: The first signature...

At the end of his article, Turgan noted that: "It
was decided recently that all pieces would bear
the small trademark shown on the accompanying
drawing. We regret that it is only on paper. We
feel that it would be much easier to engrave or
paint this mark on glass. Baccarat products
would thus, in the same way as Sèvres', carry an
indelible "stamp" which would attract the
attention of buyers.

Paper label
1860 - 1936

The first trademark represented a decanter,
contained in a circle, flanked by a stemmed glass
and a goblet above which the name of Baccarat
was printed. It was registered on October 29,
1860 at the Clerk's Office of the Paris
Commercial Court. Unfortunately, as Turgan
pointed out, this paper label was not enough
since it was immediately removed once the
object had been purchased. In 1875, Baccarat's
name appeared in relief on the molded pieces,
written in block letters. The bronze mountings
produced by Baccarat also bore a signature. It
was not until the twentieth century that all
pieces coming out of the crystal factory bore an
engraved signature. Initially affixed to scent
bottles in the twenties, it was systematically put
on the entire product range, except lighting, as of
1936. This acid engraving, called "thumb-
engraving," was replaced by sand-blasting in
1971. Since 1990, a laser-written Baccarat
signature has gradually been added to the old
mark representing the decanter, stemmed glass
and goblet, except on jewelry.

Acid-etched trademark on perfume bottle

circa **1920**

Signature for molded pieces

circa **1870**

Acid-etched or sandblasted trademark

since **1936**

Baccarat

Laser signature completing the engraved trademark

since **1990**

Baccarat on the Champ de Mars:
the 1867 World Fair

The World's Fair which opened in Paris in 1867 dazzlingly marked the end of the splendors of the "Imperial Feast". It covered 140,000 meters square, i.e., a surface area four times greater than in 1855. It attracted seven million visitors who were able to discover the latest technological marvels assembled in the imposing palace built on the Champ de Mars, and the first "exotic" pavillions: Egyptian temple, the Bey of Tunis' Palace and even a Mexican temple. Japan was also represented with a wide selection of objects; the simplicity of their shapes and decorations seemed out of place compared with the eclectism of the Europeans.

Baccarat was magnificiently represented, notably by a fountain 7.30 meters high, supporting two superimposed basins, the diameter of the larger one measuring 3.10 meters. Strangely, no trace remains of this monumental piece today.

As a testament to engraver J.-B. Simon's virtuosity, a pair of covered vases in clear crystal cased in ruby-colored crystal commanded the jury's admiration. Each included a central medallion reproducing a painting by Charles Natoire (the eighteenth century painter and engraver), which found its inspiration in mythology. The first, "Water Allegory" depicted Poseidon, god of the Seas, together with his wife, Amphitrite, on the opposite side, reclining and surrounded by her son Triton and the Nereids. The other, "Allegory of the Earth," portrayed Cybele, goddess of fertile earth, feeding a child at the foot of a fruit tree. On the other side, the engraved theme symbolizes the abundance of earthly food. Each allegory is magnified by the presence of animals living underwater, in the first instance, and forest dwellers, in the second. A profusion of details treated

in the Bérain manner covers both vases. Their rectangular bases are in chiseled bronze, each angle bearing a mask. The two vases are signed and dated: J.-B. Simon, engraver at Baccarat, 1867. Simon's achievement was to be honored with a special distinction.

On the subject of Baccarat, as stated in the report by the Workers' Delegations: "A great number of large pieces including two richly cut and perfectly fitted Medici vases, are proof that the great factory has reached an unprecedented degree of perfection. " The two vases, both one meter sixty high, welcomed the visitors at the entrance to the Baccarat stand. The same report alluded to "a large quantity of remarkable chandeliers, with elegant and varied shapes, which are striking for the richness of the

Drawing for a fountain

1867

Preliminary drawing of Simon vases

circa **1865**

"Water Allegory". Engraving by Jean-Baptiste Simon

1866 - 1867

"Earth Allegory". Engraving by Jean-Baptiste Simon

1866 - 1867

engravings and the purity of the crystal." These comments were made by a delegation of crystal engravers. In 1862, various trade associations had already been to the Great Exhibition in London to compare their own knowledge to that of their foreign counterparts. Following its visit, each delegation was required to write a report expressing its "wishes and needs" on technological and social issues. The reports were compiled under the title *Report by Workers' Delegations* to be published after the Exhibition.

Besides the great prestigious pieces, an array of enamelled vases, ewers, wheel or acid-etched, delicately chiseled stemware graced Baccarat's display, the only crystalworks to obtain First Prize at the Great Exhibition.

1867-1870: the end of the "Imperial Feast"

Despite the splendors of the 1867 Exhibition, France was experiencing economic and political difficulties and the "Imperial feast" seemed to be drawing to a close. Since the beginning of the 1860's, industrial growth had slowed down considerably. Encouraged by her victory over Austria at Sadowa, Bismarck's Prussia appeared to pose an increasing threat to the Empire. The Mexican expedition launched at the Emperor's behest in 1862 ended in disaster five years later. Finally, political opposition, which grouped together republicans and monarchists alike, gained ground during the 1869 elections. The social measures taken by Napoleon the Third, such as the right to strike in 1864, or the permission granted to workers to form associations, earned him the disapproval of industrialists and did not even win him support from workers, most of whom were republican. Following Bismarck's provocation,

France was forced to declare war on Prussia on July 19, 1870. The army was particularly ill-prepared and quickly put to rout. On September 1, the Emperor, surrounded in Sedan, was taken prisoner. Three days later, the Republic was proclaimed in Paris. The period following this defeat was marked by a series of tragic events between the Paris insurrection, the Commune which ended in the "bloody week" and the loss of Alsace Lorraine under the Treaty of Frankfurt signed on May 10, 1871. The same treaty compelled France to pay five billion gold-francs in reparations. This debt would be repaid two years later attesting to the country's wealth. The commitment made after the 1867 Exhibition to repeat the experience in 1878 would be kept proving that the bitter defeat of 1870 had not impaired the country's will to be in the foreground of international events.

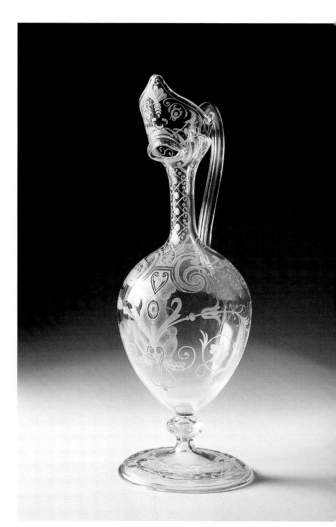

Chimaera ewer

1867

Cover of sales catalogue

The Republic
settles in...

Jean-Baptiste Toussaint's son-in-law, Paul Michaut, once deputy director of the crystalworks, was appointed deputy managing director in 1865. It was his aim to continually modernize the firm. In 1867, conclusive attempts were made to use coal gas furnaces. The process invented by Boetius, a German engineer and former student of Siemens, was adopted. Henceforth, fusion took place in closed crucibles. Boetius' furnaces would be used to equip all the *halles* until 1935. With the opening of a *flatting* workshop, glassworkers' output of stemware increased. Previously, the final stage of glassmakers' work consisted in cutting the rim or top part of glasses with shears, each glass being "open by fire". From then on, this process would take place in a workshop where glasses placed on a turntable passed in front of a blowlamp which cut the glass at the desired level. A buff wheel was then used to smooth the cut, a technique called *flatting*. Afterwards, the edges of the glass were polished by heat to prevent them from being sharp.

The crystalworks had increased its exports considerably. Company representatives were sent all over the world, and in 1865, in spite of Bohemian competition, a very large order for chandeliers was placed in Constantinople.

When the 1870 war broke out, three of the five furnaces were turned off. The 1870-71 annual report showed a sharp fall in profits but the decline was reversed in 1872 due in part to foreign sales which outstripped domestic sales. Meanwhile, the Moselle, home of Saint-Louis, had become German territory. As a result, Baccarat's ex-rival lost its French market because of the high customs duties between the two countries. Despite the Austro-German economic crash in 1873, demand was so great that a year later, Baccarat was working with seven furnaces and a staff of some two thousand. That same year, however, Paul Michaut told the Board of Directors of trade difficulties due to the crash. He advocated demand-driven production to keep inventories in line. This cautious policy would be followed until the onset of the First World War and enable Baccarat to maintain its course despite the ups and downs of the particularly turbulent economic situation during the last quarter of the nineteenth century. For all its managers' reservations, Baccarat had to be present at the 1878 Paris World Fair, to assert its superiority over other crystalworks.

Paris, 1878: The World's Fair

This first republican exhibition extended from the
Champ de Mars to the Trocadero, where a palace
was built for the occasion. Unlike the 1855 and 1867
exhibitions mainly focused on industrial progress,
this one was of a more festive nature. It included
many attractions such as the "Street of Nations" with
its picturesque facades and the aquarium in the
gardens of the Trocadero. In addition, inventions
such as Bell's telephone, invented in 1876, and
Hughes' microphone were presented.

Japanese-style vase

1878

Bowl fashioned in 1878, engraved in 1909

Coffee-pot for a Turkish set

1878

Lobed bowl
1878

Baccarat's main piece around which the whole collection revolved was a rotunda-like temple housing a "flying Mercury" in silver-plated bronze after a sculpture by Gaimbologna (i.e., Jean de Boulogne, 1524-1608), for the Medici family in Florence: the Bargello Mercury. The temple had impressive proportions (height: 4.70 m, diameter: 5.25 m) and attracted as much admiration as criticism. Some acclaimed the feat, the assembly of the different parts, the perfection of the cutting and the crystal, while others were infuriated by the use of crystal for a piece traditionally made in stone. In 1892, the King of Portugal, Don Louis, bought the temple which has been kept in a private estate close to Barcelona since 1917, where it sits imposingly in the middle of an ornamental pond. Despite the controversial points of view regarding the temple, Baccarat once again carried off the World's Fair First Prize. Among the pieces exhibited, some drew particular attention, namely those imitating sixteenth century rock crystal objects belonging to the Louvre collections. Their free shapes, perfect cutting and engraving and the purity of crystal were acclaimed unanimously. An elephant carrying a liqueur cabinet in a bronze palanquin with glasses hanging from the harness was among the most extraordinary pieces. Vases with line-engraved Japanese-like decorations were also exhibited. As of 1878, line-engraving was widely used by Baccarat. It was performed with corundum wheels much harder and bigger than the copper wheels traditionally used for engraving. The print was deeper and wider to the point of resembling cutting. It then could be polished by means of an acid-bath. In spite of the First Prize, Baccarat's managers decided to stop exhibiting in France at this type of event. Not until 1909 in Nancy did they go back on their decision. The reasons for this were multiple: even though the Exhibition report published in 1880 began the paragraph on Baccarat in the following terms: "The great house of Baccarat which France may consider to be one of her national glories, has made progress since 1867". A few lines further down, it said: "Baccarat is still lacking firm artistic direction." It is nonetheless true that the premises of what we refer to by the generic term of "decorative art" appeared at the end of the 1870's. The influence of Japan was at the root of a new esthetic current, *Japanism*: France begin to discover everyday Japanese objects in 1867. The inspiration drawn from the traditional subjects of the Middle Ages, the Renaissance or the eighteenth century contrasted with another, provided by new sources such as naturalist themes. At the same time, free shapes urged designers to "explore" areas which until then had been the reserve of industrialists. Glassworking followed the trend and the names of personalities who had created unique pieces or objects produced in small series bearing their signature appeared beside the manufactures even though such pieces had been produced industrially. Among the best known forerunners, François-Eugène Rousseau and Emile Gallé paved the way for a new glass art which would proceed well into the twentieth century. They did not represent direct competition for Baccarat. The Company remained in the foreground among crystal industrialists but the risk of being deprived of supreme recognition by a "craftsman" prompted it not to take part in this kind of contest. This decision, dictated by wisdom, was reinforced by the fact that the economic crisis showed no sign of letting up. It was more important for Baccarat to expand and guarantee her markets especially in South America and India, than face competition where there was nothing else to be proved.

Elephant liquor cabinet

1878

Decanter

1878

Punch bowl

1900

1889-1900: Baccarat's statement on social policy

In France, the second half of the nineteenth century was marked by numerous conflicts triggered by workers' social claims. From the outset, Baccarat had solved the problems that could arise as a result of discontentment in the workforce. Its directors quickly understood that only workers' loyalty could ensure the quality and "perfection" of its products. The glassmakers were the first to be awarded special status. Starting in 1823, they were accommodated in rent-free lodgings next to the *halle*, for practical reasons. From 1888 on, each house was renovated on a regular basis, and comprised a cellar, a ground floor with two rooms including a kitchen and a second floor with two bedrooms and an attic. There usually was a little garden adjoining the house. In 1827, six years before the Guizot Law on education, a school for boys was set up for workers' sons. It was also open for two hours in the evening for adults. Some forty years later, girls would have their own school. Until 1881, 1% of all wages was withheld to cover the cost of running the school, medical care and religious services.

Traditionally, in the event of illness, glassmakers received the equivalent of two-thirds of their wages.

They were also granted an annuity once they were too old to work. In 1835, a contingency fund was set up for engravers. It was funded by a 1% levy on wages and the proceeds of fines punishing poor quality work or behavior contrary to the rules. The fund was regularly in deficit and bailed out by the Company's special donations. In the event of illness, an engraver who was off work for more than three days, drew half his wages. However, engravers felt frustrated when comparing their lot with glassmakers. In 1840, a semblance of a strike broke out, the only one Baccarat has ever known. The cutters' working conditions were particularly hard: the atmosphere in the cutting workshops was very humid and handling tin ash caused a great many lung diseases. As of 1844, during winter, hot water was used to run the lathes and the workshops were better equipped with heating and lighting.

Before the 1851 Law was passed setting up a national pension fund, most of Baccarat's workers, glassmakers and engravers were already drawing a pension when they stopped working. The amount granted to them depended on the management's goodwill. Made official in 1850, the engravers' fund was financed by the Company and covered "any worker over fifty who has worked a minimum of twenty consecutive years at the factory and is recognized as unable to continue performing his job." Workers were also entitled to place their savings with the Company which paid them 4 to 5% interest. The savings fund appears to date from 1831 and ceased operation in 1881.

The various funds were managed by boards of directors and included a number of elected workers. As of 1860, the female workforce began to increase in number. Women employed in the *flatting* and gilding workshops and in the packaging shops were

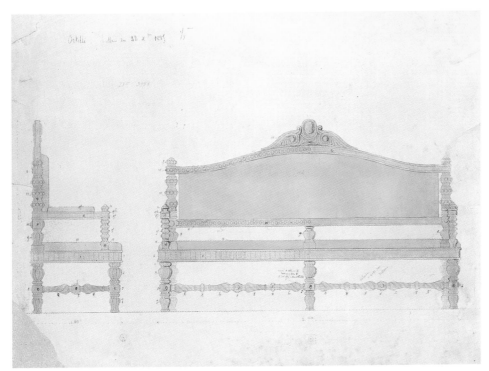

Furniture drawing
1885

paid less than men and were not entitled to the benefits of any contingency fund. It was only in 1896 that they would win entitlement to a form of assistance in the event of illness or unemployment: i.e., a personal "passbook" into which the equivalent of 3% of their wages was paid each month, including 1% paid by the Company. From 1823, in comparison with other categories of French workers, Baccarat's workforce enjoyed considerably higher pay than the national average. Further, the crystalworks' social institutions were exemplary in the context of the nineteenth century. As early as 1867 they earned the Company a gold medal awarded by the Society for the Protection of Apprentices and Children of the Manufactures, on the occasion of the World's Fair.

In November 1887, a letter written on Ministry of Commerce and Industry letterhead was sent to Adrien Michaut who had replaced his father as the Company's managing director in 1883. The future director of the 1889 Exhibition was concerned when he saw that Baccarat's name did not feature in category 19 (crystal, glass and stained glass). He urged Adrien Michaut to participate: "my strongest and most patriotic desire is to see your factory, so well-known worldwide, and located on our eastern border, where national pride is so strong, stronger than elsewhere, prepare to send us a selection of your finest products in 1889." Four days later, Baccarat's reply was quite clear: "The Baccarat Crystalworks Company shareholders' council, after deliberation at its meeting of September 21, 1886, has decided not to take part in the 1889 World's Fair." The end of the letter explained this refusal: "We believe that we can more firmly ensure the industrial power and commercial prosperity of our company by allocating the considerable sums that such an exhibition would cost us, at a loss, on improving and expanding our

Iris vase

1900

behind the decision. His social convictions prompted him to want to establish close relations between workers and managers. His opinions were extremely "avant-garde" for the time. He even came up with the idea of an employers' council elected by workers under universal suffrage to manage the Company. The idea was rejected by the Board of Directors. When he died, in 1899, eight of the fifty nine shares he owned were left to the Crystalworks' workers who would divide the interest between themselves every year. He also had an important role in founding the Social Museum of Paris.

In 1900 Baccarat once again refused to take part directly in the exhibition, although the Company was present in the Social Economy section. It was awarded two major prizes for its remuneration policy and the contingency institutions it provided plus two silver medals recognizing the treatment of apprentices and workers' accommodations.

A sumptuous piece from the Crystalworks, symbolizing the City of Paris, was however exhibited at the very famous Paris store, *Le Grand*

equipment and setting up offices in faraway places to show our products to - and bring them within the reach of - consumers who would not otherwise know of our existence despite all our success in Paris. This attitude was all the more reasonable as many foreign visitors to the exhibition went to the Crystalworks showroom on rue de Paradis where sales increased spectacularly that same year. Although it did not exhibit any objects, Baccarat did take part in the Exhibition of Social Economy where it was awarded First Prize for its institutions in support of its 2,025 workers. After the event, the Board of Directors decided to set up an unemployment fund. The Comte de Chambrun, the Company's main shareholder by his marriage to one of Godard-Desmarest's daughters, was probably

Adrien Michaut

Table and Boat (Reproduced in 1989)

1889   1900

Dépôt (The large showroom). In his book entitled *La verrerie à l'exposition universelle de 1900* (Glassware at the 1900 World's Fair) published in 1902, Jules Henrivaux described "a huge crystal vessel on a molded and engraved base with its bowl engraved on raw material with diamond strings, and chiselled and gilded bronze ornaments, a piece by the sculptor Cornu (produced in Baccarat's factories)."
Contrary to what had happened in 1889, the shop on rue de Paradis did not increase its sales during the exhibition.

Pair of vases

1900

The end of an area

The beginning of the century brought important changes within Baccarat. Since 1898, a telephone line linking the factory and the town of Lunéville, connected in turn to Paris, enabled the Paris showroom and the crystal factory to communicate with one another.

The layout of the Paris warehouse was modernized in order to widen the clientele of wholesalers and merchants to include direct sales. The walls were repainted and the wooden floors covered with linoleum, a new material only recently introduced in France. In 1908, living rooms were fitted out in accordance with the wish expressed at the board meeting held in September of that year: "We cannot show customers our electric lighting fixtures in proper conditions which would allow them to appreciate the fixtures effect in the environment where they should be set up. This shortcoming impairs sales and we have decided to make up for it by fitting out living rooms with proportions similar to those usually found in bourgeois apartments where lighting fixtures and art pieces will eventually be displayed." The Crystalworks also changed appearance. New workers' lodgings were built right up until the war, and after 1912, automobiles replaced the horses used for making deliveries, gradually eliminating the need for stables.

Starting in the 1890's, the Crystalworks had a serious recruitment problem which became crucial at the beginning of the twentieth century. In 1901 most of the *gamins* taken in by the crystal factory's boarding house came from Brittany since the Meurthe and Vosges areas were then experiencing an industrial boom which deprived Baccarat of potential manpower for the future. The factory was not able to honor all its orders for want of staff. Efforts were made to mechanize certain production

Rhine wine glass
1904

Ink pot

circa **1903**

techniques, such as engraving and stopping
perfumers' bottles, an industry which was
developing at an outstanding rate.

Perfumers' bottles

A new cutting workshop was built in 1907 about ten
miles from Baccarat in the vicinity of Rambervilliers.
It employed women exclusively, recruited locally for
cutting stoppers and perfume bottles mechanically.
Initially, the workshop produced 4,000 bottles a day.
As underscored in the Board of Directors' report of
1907: "The crystal perfume bottle industry is very
young. Ten years ago, we were not delivering more
than 150 items a day...."
After a year's apprenticeship, the cutting workshop's
143 female workers were operational. The demand
for bottles was on the increase requiring the
workshop to be expanded four years later to produce
5,000 bottles a day. The largest orders were placed
by the perfumer François Coty and by Houbigant.
Guerlain, whose first orders dated back to the Second
Empire, came out in 1912 with the famous bottle
whose stopper was shaped as a *gendarme*'s hat, the

guardian of renowned fragrances such as "Fol
Arôme," "Mitsouko" and "L'Heure Bleue". Even
during the war, after only a few months of lying idle,
Rambervilliers started work again with large orders
from Coty, to name but one. Economic recovery,
once the war was over, helped the perfume and
bottle industries to expand. The names of perfumers
were soon joined by famous couturiers such as Paul
Poiret or Jean Patou whose bottles for "Amour
Amour" (1924) and "Normandie" (1935-1940) were
designed by Louis Süe, co-founder, with André
Mare, of the *Compagnie des Arts Français*. In 1925,
Georges Chevalier, Baccarat's appointed designer,
designed a bottle for the perfumer Lubin in the shape
of two dolphins joined at their heads and tails.
Production was increased over the years notably by
the bottles designed for Elisabeth Arden including in
1939 the famous hand clasping the perfume bottle
"It's You', or those produced for Schiaparelli, of

"Le Roy Soleil"

1945

"Mitsouko"

1912

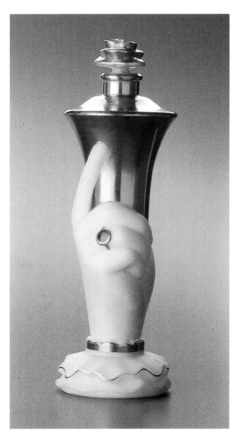

"It's you"

1939

which the most famous was "Le Roy Soleil" designed in 1945 by Dali. The creations for Christian Dior from "Diorama" in 1949 to "Eau Sauvage Extrême" in 1966, punctuated each of the couturier's essences. The 1980's were marked by bottles designed for Paco Rabanne such as "Calandre," or for Gianni Versace for whom the designer Thierry Lecoule created the bottle and presentation box for the perfume "V'e Versace," which was awarded the City of Paris' First Prize for Creation in 1989.

Many of the shapes initially produced in crystal by Baccarat have been taken up by glasshouses at the request of perfumers because of cost restrictions. The bottles produced by the Crystalworks bear the Baccarat trademark which was initially acid-etched, during the twenties then acid-etched or sandblasted from 1936 on.

Baccarat and its manpower: a crisis?

While recruiting female employees allowed Baccarat to meet the demand for perfume bottles, it did not however solve the problems of staff shortages whether it be of glassmakers, engravers or apprentices. An attractive wage policy introduced in 1907 bore fruit the following year with regular raises prompting workers to stay at the Crystalworks. The acute recruitment crisis seemed to have been resolved: within a year, the workforce rose from 2,115 workers and employees in 1907 to 2,226 in 1908. At the meeting of the Board of Directors in September 1911, Adrien Michaut proposed a plan to back the construction of new lodgings for future engravers: "To settle interesting prospects after their military service, we believe that nothing would be more efficient than comfortable accommodations provided cheaply." He concluded: "The industrial training of a large number of apprentices is an

expense without immediate compensation." Work
began on building the lodgings that very year
followed by the expansion of the apprentices'
accommodations due to the increased number of
gamins.

1909, Nancy: International Exhibition in Eastern France
1910, Paris: Exhibition of Art Glassware and Crystalware at the Galliera Museum

Bolstered by its commercial success in France and
abroad, Baccarat took part in the great exhibition of
1909 in Nancy. Its managing director, Adrien
Michaut, was Chairman of the Jury for class VII
objects which covered construction and decoration,
as well as furniture for public buildings and private
accommodations. The Crystalworks was declared
ineligible for this category but the Company's
magnificent stand earned it a special prize: the
Département (administrative division) prize. The
jury's report describes its display in the following
terms: "...we are stunned by the matchless mastery
which went into shaping and decorating the crystal."
Saint-Louis Crystalworks was also present. Although
attached geographically to the German Empire, it
was still managed by a Frenchman. The School of
Nancy's Pavillion was host to the house of Daum,
which started producing art pieces in 1890, and the
house of Gallé, managed by Emile Gallé's son-in-law
after Gallé's death in 1904.
Although sales made during the exhibition far from
covered the expenses incurred, Baccarat's
management was delighted at having taken part in
the event: "The success of our stand has been as
complete as we could have hoped for. We were
awarded two medals of honor given in the name of

Rhine wine glass
1909

the Département to the most prestigious exhibits."
The following year, a retrospective focusing on
thirty years of glass creation was organized at Paris'
Galliera museum. Next to the greatly prestigious
items, gilded services, richly enamelled chalices
reminiscent of Islamic glassware, engraved vases
including Petrement's and line-engraved bowls,
Baccarat exhibited a series of sixteen glasses from the
Gala stemware produced for the French Presidency
and foreign courts, a tradition dating back to the
beginning of the Crystalworks with the stemware
made for Louis XVIII.
Noteworthy exhibitors included René Lalique as
well as various glassmakers working single-handedly
in their own workshops: François Décorchemont,
Albert Dammouse and Georges Despret.
An article by Maurice Guillemot published in the
magazine *Arts et Decoration* in 1910, while criticizing
some of the shapes exhibited by Baccarat, did
acknowledge that "it is fair to praise the cutting and
engraving work. The refinement of the work is

exceptional, the wheel is just as subtle as an etcher's burin or a point, the circle of antique figurines has incredible lightness, finesse and delicacy."

Domestic and foreign markets

During this time, the Baccarat Company strove to find new markets. Production of perfumers' bottles had given access to a buoyant industry and the concomitant financial returns. The Paris showroom, after faring moderately until 1905 due to economic instability, saw its sales increase steadily until the war mainly due to direct sales. Department stores such as Le Louvre, Le Bon Marché, Le Printemps and Galeries Lafayette were also selling numerous toilet articles as well as reasonably priced stemware which attracted a large clientele. Finally, luxury hotels and various railway and shipping companies regularly repeated their orders. The only fly in the ointment remained the desperately weak provincial market. Foreign markets however were growing. Weakened by unforeseen events such as the Russo-Japanese war of 1904-1905 and the cholera epidemic in Italy in 1911, these markets had to be expanded in order to be profitable. The role of agents working on the spot and "travelers" prospecting potential markets then became decisive. In 1904, one traveler began a tour which took him to the British colonies of the Cape and Australia, the Republic of Argentina, Brazil, Mexico and Cuba. In the next two years, sales in Argentina and Brazil rose considerably. Whenever a market seemed promising, an agency or a warehouse was set up in that country. The Company relied entirely on the skills of the agent working in the sales territory. In 1907, the New York agent was fired because of bad management and the few orders he had attracted. The time it took to replace him and set sales rolling again meant as many months lost for the

"Johannisberg" bottle
1887

Chalice
1909

Company. In Europe, the 'conquest' of England still remained a problem. Despite opening a shop in London on Bond Street in 1909, bringing together French industries such as Christofle, Haviland and Baccarat under one roof, sales were still slow. Despite ups and downs from one year to the next, a hotel network spread throughout Italy which relied on the Baccarat crystalworks. Germany constantly increased its orders in particular for engraved stemware and perfume bottles. In 1913, the Board of Directors' report described relations between Baccarat and Germany as follows: "We consider the results to be satisfactory given the recession which has hit Germany more so than elsewhere and the commercial nationalism that is fighting French imports into this country." The same year, the achievements of the Russia and Orient agency were, as in 1912, exceptionally good. Relations between Baccarat and Russia dated back to the end of the nineteenth century,when, in 1896, 3.85-meter-high candelabras were ordered by Tsar Nicolas the Second for his palace in St. Petersburg. The candelabras were displayed for the first time at the 1878 exhibition. They then bore 79 wax candles. However the models made for the Tsar used electricity. Another candelabra was produced on this occasion for the Tsarina after a design dating from 1867. From 1896 onwards, the substantial number of orders placed, ranging from lighting fixtures to stemware to which small vodka glasses were added, required full-time use of a furnace which came to be known as "the Russian furnace." Transportation was by mule teams laden with crystal leaving Baccarat for distant Russia. From this sumptuous era remain, besides the famous "Tsar's glasses," two candelabras kept in the Baccarat museum on the rue de Paradis, as the First World War, followed by the 1917 Revolution, had prevented their delivery.

In 1905, the Shah of Persia's visit to Paris seemed to be a good omen for reviving this market which had declined since the extraordinary purchases made by Shah Nasr Ed Din in 1873. The inventory included a 2.15-meter-high candelabra (a copy of which still greets visitors today at the rue du Paradis), a great many stemware patterns as well as opalines of all sizes.

Unfortunately, although substantial orders were placed in 1905, the Company would have great difficulty getting paid for them. On the brink of war, Baccarat asserted its position as a model industry for the incomparable quality and diversity of its products, for its social institutions which ensured it a highly qualified workforce as well as for its conquest of domestic and foreign markets.

Tsar's stemware

1909

Tsar's candelabra

circa `1896`

"Perfection," the Company watchword launched in 1823 by Pierre-Antoine Godard-Desmarest, had been scrupulously respected throughout the ninety-year period. From 1912 on, the first premonitory signs of a serious international crisis began to loom on the horizon. Markets got carried away to such an extent that year that Adrien Michaut indicated in his report to shareholders that "the abundance of orders received has been abnormal". The feeling of insecurity between Germany and France was compounded along the borders of eastern France with, notably, the construction in Baccarat of barracks to accommodate a garrison of 3,000 men. In 1912, war was raging in the Balkan Peninsula. All these factors were signs of the future 1914-1918 conflict which broke out between France and Germany on August 3, 1914 marking the "end of an era" once and for all.

Baccarat during the war

On August 2, 1914, as mobilization had deprived the Crystalworks of three-quarters of its glassmakers, three out of the four furnaces were turned off. Only some of the cutting workshops were kept running to finish the crystal already made. Others, including Rambervilliers, were put completely out of work and compensation was paid to the workforce. A makeshift mill was set up to ensure flour supplies. On August 24, at night, following the retreat of French troops defeated at Sarrebourg, the Germans stormed into Baccarat after bombing the town. The apprentices' lodgings and workers' accommodations were set on fire by enemy shells. The day after, a French shell landed on the *halle* destroying the only furnace still working. A few days later on September 12, their setback in the famous Battle of the Marne forced the Germans to retreat after burning down on

their way a cutting workshop, workers' accommodations, and the acid-engraving workshop. Numerous thefts of equipment and crystal pieces testified to their passing through the area. French battalions gained the lost ground they were defending by digging trenches, some of them east of Baccarat. Until March, the Crystalworks lived in fear of the return of the enemy, in which case it had been decided that both the factory and its surroundings would be destroyed so that the Germans would not be able to take shelter in them. At the beginning of 1915, work gradually picked up again. There was no shortage of raw materials or fuel, and communications had been restored, more particularly, the railways were back in working order for transporting goods. Hope returned even though the furnaces and cutting workshops were running again with workers who had either been declared unfit or too old for military service. In 1915 Adrien Michaut asked the Company's shareholders to forego their profits. "This painful ordeal, the end of which is not in sight, will seem less hard if you think of the risk over several months of total destruction of the factory, which, compared with the sacrifice we are asking from you, would have been a disaster leading to the ruin of a whole generation."

Despite the international crisis which affected most markets, Baccarat continued to sell its products. In 1914, however, a fire had destroyed the London office and the Berlin one had been sequestered. The New York market remained of little importance. On the other hand, sales to Russia, Italy, Spain and Portugal continued to rise.

While the situation was tragic on France's eastern border where the very bloody trench war dragged on, Baccarat kept out of the conflict despite the presence of German trenches just ten miles from the town. The factory continued producing despite alerts and even stepped up productivity. In 1915, the perfumer François Coty placed an order for bottles for an unprecedented amount in the Company's history. In 1916, two furnaces, each with twenty crucibles, were running. The Paris market stayed afloat due to sales of perfume bottles and the recovery by department stores, Bon Marché in particular. Arrangements were made with railway companies and in exchange, the Crystalworks was granted permission to transport the raw materials needed for production. Abroad, sales in Spain kept improving, whereas Italy had recently prohibited all crystal imports. All shipping to America was postponed because of the serious dangers incurred on the seas as a consequence of the war. The war ended in April 1918 but Baccarat was threatened with evacuation in the event of German offensives. As a precautionary measure, the factory's management decided to hide all plans and models as well as specimens of each machine in a safe place. Coal was saved where possible and one furnace was turned off. All shipping to Paris was suspended for one month. The Crystalworks did, however, manage to survive while continuing to pay its workers unemployment compensation. Even during these particularly difficult times, the demand for perfume bottles kept increasing, thanks to both Coty and Houbigant. On November 11, 1918, the armistice was finally signed putting an end to the first war in modern times.

Baccarat/Christofle Pavillion

1925

Between the wars

1919 - 1939

The first years following the war were marked at Baccarat by a new recruitment crisis. The contribution of the heavy and bloody tribute to the war had deprived the factory of a fifth of its young workers who never came back from the battlefields. Among the survivors, many would never be able to go back to work. Coty then decided to open a glass factory and a cutting workshop in the Paris area and tried to take workers away from Baccarat and Rambervilliers by offering them wages twice as high. The reconstruction sites, offering high wages, also attracted local young people. The Company reacted immediately to the circumstances: raises were given to all categories of the workforce and the construction of new workers' accommodations was soon underway. Despite breaking off with Coty, production of perfume bottles was resumed with Houbigant, Grenoville, d'Orsay and Guerlain. The market extended to Germany with Wolff, as well as Mülhens, the manufacturer of the famous Cologne no. 4711. England, which had been a problem market up until that time, also increased its orders for perfume bottles. The events of October 1917 put an end to the fabulous orders from the Russian princes and relegated the "Russian furnace" to the realm of memory of a bygone age. In 1919, by ratifying the 18th amendment of their constitution, the United States instituted prohibition banning all sales of alcohol. For Baccarat, the effect was immediate: the market for stemware in North America was reduced to nothing.

In 1920 the Company's shareholders decided to divide the initial 15,000 franc shares into six shares of 2,500 francs apiece. The amount of shares went up from 400 to 2,400.

September 28, 1922 marked the end of the Company's 100th fiscal year. The centenary was celebrated in June 1922, at the Baccarat Crystalworks. It gave the opportunity to award medals to thirty employees who had worked for the Company for over fifty years. Adrien Michaut delivered a moving speech tracing the history of the Crystalworks. Addressing himself to the crowd from the site in front of the *halles*, unchanged to this day, he said: "The old chestnut trees under which so many generations of children, including mine, have played have been succeeded by sycamore trees. It is still the same courtyard with its old chapel, the focus of the family life of the glassmakers, foremen, managing director and director, and the center of the factory's activities too. It characterizes Baccarat by the close and constant contact between workers and management." He concluded his speech by adding: "Let us say goodbye to the Baccarat of the past and salute the Baccarat of the future!"

Georges Chevalier: designer

This future, the future of "modernity," was personified by a young designer, Georges Chevalier (1894-1987), to whom Baccarat opened its doors in 1916. In 1909, Chevalier registered at the Ecole Nationale Supérieure des Arts Décoratifs (National School of Advanced Decorative Arts) in Paris. Three years later, he met the decorator Maurice Dufrêne who introduced him into his studio and under whose leadership he would create, from 1921 onwards, models for Galeries Lafayette's *Maîtrise,* the department store's creative agency. At the end of the war in 1918, another encounter allowed him to develop while creating for the Paris of the "Roaring Twenties": he met Leon Bakst, whose creations of decors and costumes for Serge de Diaghilev's Ballets Russes would be a fortunate influence on the artistic life of Paris during the first quarter of the twentieth century. It was in Baccarat, however, that Chevalier would express his talent with the most success. Although he brought a new source of inspiration to the Crystalworks, the latter did provide him with its best workers. The International Exhibition of Modern Decorative and Industrial Arts held in Paris in 1925 gave irrefutable proof of this. Initially planned for 1915, but postponed several times because of the 1914-18 war, the Exhibition finally opened in April 1925 on the Esplanade of the Invalides around the Grand Palais and on a portion of the quays either side of the Seine. Although the venue was the same as for the previous Great Exhibitions, the event had a totally different purpose. The objective was clear: any recollection of the past was banned. As Yvonne Brunhammer points out in her book entitled *1925:* "1925 was the meeting point of two "arts de vivre," one inherited from the past, the other turned towards the future which promised

Baccarat/Christofle Pavillion

1925

to be radically different, although nobody really knew what it would be like. Everybody was thus free to innovate."

For Baccarat, this exhibition was a sort of challenge. We should remember the criticism leveled after the 1878 Exhibition: the quality of craftsmanship was praised but the reports deplored the lack of artistic direction.

By entrusting Georges Chevalier with realization of the Pavillion designed to accommodate Baccarat and Christofle, the Crystalworks banked on the innovative impetus brought by this talented designer. The "harsh" critic Gabriel Mourey developed his impressions in the issue of *L'Art Vivant* (Living Art) published on May 15, 1925: "In a setting as unimposing as possible in order to give the works exhibited their full value, the most magical harmony of "silver and crystal" one could dream of was displayed." All of Georges Chevalier's talent came to the foreground around the theme of water. A magnificent chandelier, 2.80m high and 2m wide, symbolized a waterfall above a table where a glass pattern entitled "Fountains" was laid out. A copy of this chandelier was made for Sydney's Theatre Royal. Among the pieces designed by Georges Chevalier, a stem pattern entitled "For Yachting" was highly successful. The glasses' square

Georges Chevalier
"Woman in a hammock"
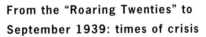
1929

hand ... gives the tone and the emotion. Why is a glass, manufactured in a hurry, cold? Why does one that is shaped slowly and beautifully, heated again, remodeled, produce such a lovely sound? If Georges Chevalier's pieces come out so alive from Baccarat's workshops, it is because they first of all are pleasing to the Lorraine workers in love with their work, who are ultimately the first critics, the first judges, and the first admirers of the young artist's creations. Until the end of the seventies, Georges Chevalier would untiringly create new shapes for Baccarat. His work, while respecting the Crystalworks' "traditional heritage" inscribed Baccarat's name on the modernity of the twentieth century.

From the "Roaring Twenties" to September 1939: times of crisis

The 1925 Exhibition portrayed the image of a festive Paris, capital of the world, trying to forget the horrors of the First World War by drowning its sorrows in new music, new fashions, new decors, and high speed. The carefree atmosphere of the "Roaring Twenties" did not quite manage to conceal the new crises which came one after the other both in France and abroad on the economic, political and social front and which would ultimately lead to the terrible conflict of 1939.

1922 marked the beginning of a series of drastic falls in the value of the French Franc. Adrien Michaut refers to them in his report on the 1925-1926 fiscal year, mentioning the effects on the price of raw materials which had quadrupled in three years. However, the products of the Crystalworks continued to be in such demand that the construction of an additional facility Baccarat was considered in Ille et Vilaine (Brittany), in the vicinity of Redon. The directors thought that it would allow

base gave them perfect stability. The Prince of Wales ordered several services of this kind for his ships with enamelled incrustations of different colors according to purpose: red for yachts, blue to honor the presence of Navy officers aboard, white for royal ships.

Over the years, Georges Chevalier enriched Baccarat's production considerably. From 1926 on, he produced a bestiary, the novelty of which opened a new door for the Crystalworks'sculpture. Georges Chevalier's strength lay in the way he worked with Baccarat's glassworkers and engravers as a team. Ernest Tisserand described this partnership in an article devoted to the art of crystal published in *Art Vivant* in October 1929:

"In any good crystal factory, the worker's skill and personality are also important. Baccarat still has the most remarkable workers. Machines and mechanization have not in any way replaced the glassblower's ability, virtuosity, and intelligence. The mold is no more than a guide, a control device. The

them to compensate for the labor shortage which had worsened since the end of the war. In 1929, Redon started work with one furnace fitted with six crucibles staffed by young workers trained by Baccarat's glassworkers. But 1929 was a bleak year marked by the Wall Street crashes of October 4 and 29 the repercussions of which reached Europe two years later.

"As a luxury and export industry, we are amongst the hardest hit in the wake of the world economic crisis." These are the words used by Adrien Michaut in 1931 to announce the overall drop in business to the Company's shareholders. It led to layoffs in the cutting and engraving workshops. The following year the situation worsened forcing the Company to cut all wages and salaries by 10%. As far as the workforce's reaction was concerned, the managing director indicated that "the former accepts without complaining the measures it understands to be necessary". In a period characterized by social unrest punctuated by innumerable strikes and take-overs of factories, the mutual trust between the workforce and Baccarat's management was exceptional. The scarcity of orders led to Redon's being closed down in 1934. After fifty-three years at the head of the Crystalworks, Adrien Michaut died in August 1936; the appointment of his son-in-law, Jean de Poncin as managing director was confirmed, and the chairmanship of the Board of Directors fell to Jacques Parisot. With the signature of the Matignon agreements between employers and trade unions on June 7, 1936, two weeks' paid annual vacation as well as a forty-hour work-week were instituted. These new social measures were put into practice the following year creating some concern among company managers, all the more so since the Franc was devalued in September. In Baccarat's case, the problem of vacations was a tricky one since it was

"Majestic" stemware
1929

"Champs Elysées" stemware

1934

"Aurèle de Paladines" stemware

1937

Since 1936, the remilitarization of the Rhineland undertaken by Hitler had aroused legitimate concern. On May 15, 1939, when German troops invaded Bohemia, war seemed inevitable. It was declared jointly by England and France on September 3, 1939, two days after the invasion of Poland by Hitler's army.

Stemware n° 14

1937

impossible to turn off the furnaces for two weeks, a forty-day period being necessary to fire them up again. So it was decided that the workers would take their vacations in rotation. The fall of the Franc encouraged exports as would be confirmed by the profits recorded for the 1937 fiscal year.

The end of the year was marked by worldwide economic recovery, capped in 1937 by the International Exhibition of Arts and Techniques in Paris. Baccarat displayed a series of stemware for the table as well as for cocktails, salad bowls, vases, toiletry sets, etc. The emphasis was put on the purity and transparency of the crystal and free forms. From the muslin crystal, so thin as to be a mere suggestion, to crystal structured in its thickness by engraving, the range of pieces presented by Baccarat fit in with the modernity of the exhibition which was open to artists and industrialists alike.

The eagle atop the German pavillion facing a Russian couple holding a hammer and sickle and the presence of Picasso's "Guernica" in the Spanish pavillion appeared as premonitions of an uncertain future.

The bleak years

1939 - 1945

Baccarat had just pulled out of the economic crisis when the conflict broke out. Its order books were full due to the export market, with particularly good results in Central and South America. Its participation in the French pavillion at the New York World's Fair was an attempt to establish itself in the United States. Special stemware had been produced or adapted to American customs with much larger glasses to accommodate the ice cubes that Americans so often mix with their drinks. The American boycott of products from Germany and Czechoslovakia appeared to bode well for the Crystalworks. Although the French market remained weak for stemware as well as prestigious items, an increasing number of large orders placed by Guerlain as well as Elizabeth Arden, Schiaparelli and Corday justified full employment of the workforce. The participation of Baccarat, with Georges Chevalier, in the 1939 Decorators & Artists Exhibition in Paris was a success confirmed by numerous orders.

These satisfactory results led to a third furnace being fired up in March. On September 3, however, the factory once again lost its young workers, called back to arms by the general mobilization. Just as the time before, the Crystalworks continued to operate with the help of workers too old to fight in the war, and women.

Georges Chevalier - Glass exhibited at the Artists-Decorators Exhibition

1939

"On June 17 (1940), the Germans invaded Baccarat and immediately transformed the factory into a vast camp housing 25,000 prisoners. Our old workers who had stayed at home were brutally expelled in the middle of the night and the German flag was hoisted up over the buildings."

This is how the direct consequences of the French armed forces' defeat at Baccarat were described in the minutes of the Board of Directors meeting, on

Stemware n° 15 exhibited in New York in 1939

1937

October 22, 1940. The factory was occupied for two months and suffered many acts of depredation, although some of the molds had been buried in time to be spared from theft.

Baccarat directors' main concern then was to ensure the survival of the Crystalworks during the hostilities. However, the fact that industries were suddenly put under the administrative supervision of various ministries soon proved to be a daily burden, due to the inefficiency of the civil servants in charge of implementing governmental policies that would constantly contradict each other until the end of the war. Baccarat was placed under the aegis of the Ministry of Trade and almost had to turn off its furnaces for lack of fuel. Not knowing that these furnaces had to be fed with coal, the government official in charge refused to have the fuel delivered. To be able to continue functioning, Baccarat started manufacturing radio tubes, which allowed the Company to get coal sparingly. Life at the factory remained geared to the future, i.e., towards the end of the conflict. In anticipation, the Paris showroom had put away all recently produced modern items and taken out its old stock to guarantee sales after the war.

In Baccarat the factory strove to recruit local young men thereby sparing them "compulsory labor" (S.T.O) in Germany. However, from one month to the next the situation became more and more tragic. The scarcity of food supplies was then one of the population's main concerns, as stated in the Board of Directors report in May 1942: "There is no doubt that our young workers are physically exhausted mainly because, on top of their regular jobs, they have to search for food supplies. The meager results thus obtained do not compensate, most of the time, for the effort involved." The factory did, however, rent a piece of land to grow potatoes, but the

Stemware N°2 exhibited in New York in 1939

1937

suffering due to malnutrition would last until the end of the war.

Despite hindrances, such as the ban on making crystal other than for export, Baccarat's furnaces were in operation and the factory stored raw crystal which would give work to the cutting workshops in better days. Hope never failed. In 1943, the factory's management mentioned in its bi-annual report that henceforth the Crystalworks would aim towards improving equipment: "Good workers should be equipped with proper tools ...." That same year, the drain on manpower for the S.T.O. and the State could not be avoided. A small contingent of older glassmakers remained at the site: "...it would be vainly ambitious to try to increase our workforce appreciably at a time when the country is being systematically deprived of its men and the State is draining off the minute proportion of available

mainpower into comfortable, well-paid positions."
Difficulties were mounting: minium became
impossible to find, coal was distributed more and
more sparsely, and the factory had very few workers
left. Yet hope remained strong.

In 1944, confusion was at its peak: "Although
through more or less official channels we hear from
all sides that the French economy, wages and social
matters are being put in order, we are actually seeing
on the economic, social and technical front the worst
confusion and disorder that France has ever known.
We have reached the logical outcome of an
experiment with a head-less state-controlled
economy. Keeping the factory running was an uphill
struggle, as survival depended on fluctuating coal
deliveries and manpower. The report then specified
that "management overburdens the facilities as much
as it can, but no one is concerned with maintaining
sufficient control over French industry to allow it to
start up again quickly after the war..."

Since 1939 every Board of Directors report
mentioned the end of the war, hoping for it,
imagining it in the near future. All decisions were
motivated by these expectations as well as all
sacrifices, whether from the management or the
workforce.

Finally, on June 6, 1944, the Allies landed on the
Normandy coast. Paris was liberated on August 25,
although the war would not end until the following
year with the German surrender on May 8, 1945.

In 1944, the furnaces were turned off. Only the
cutting workshops were in operation: they processed
the raw crystal accumulated throughout the years.
Soon Baccarat found itself in the last firing line,
completely cut off from the rest of the country. From
September 28 to October 31, the town was caught in
the midst of heavy fighting between the Germans
and the Allies, the Gestapo sowing terror in the
town.

Bombing destroyed the church and the surrounding
areas, killing a dozen people. The *halles,* the workers'
lodgings, the nursery and the *Château* were hit by
shelling and torpedoes. Twenty-five shells landed on
the Rambervilliers factory.

The available stock was hidden away in a terrible
rush. Two weeks later, Baccarat was finally
liberated. Work resumed progressively at the
Crystalworks, first in the cutting workshops and a
month later around the furnaces. Production was
started up again with a high proportion of new
items. As in the past, events adverse to its destiny had
not harmed the Crystalworks' desire to survive at all
costs.

From recovery to consecration

In France, the years following the end of the war were marked by enormous political difficulties, with a succession of short-lived governments, and economically, with the disastrous fluctuations of the Franc. Baccarat had several priorities, the main one being, as in the past, to rebuild an elite workforce. In 1945, the factory employed 600 people; a year later, staffing levels reached 800. All efforts focused on improving working conditions and raising wages. It was also necessary to revive foreign markets, reduced to nothing by the end of the war.

In 1948, with his young wife, Josée, René de Chambrun, son of General de Chambrun, the Crystalworks vice-president, and Aldebert de Chambrun's great nephew, created a wholesale and retail shop in New York. The following year the results already seemed promising. Although the European market had shrunk considerably following the Yalta agreements due to the exclusion of the "Eastern Block," the South American market, on the other hand, was in expansion. It was not until 1950 that the difficult hurdle of reconstruction would be over.

In 1951, the Museum of Decorative Arts in Paris organized an international exhibition devoted to the art of glass. Baccarat was represented in the contemporary section by a majority of pieces designed by Georges Chevalier including the "Maladetta" stemware. Next to the modern items, a retrospective recounting the history of glass in

Georges Chevalier- "Maladetta" stemware

1951

France was presented for which about forty Baccarat pieces, dating from 1823 to 1925, were selected. Despite the seriousness of the French economic situation, Baccarat consolidated its sales abroad. The Company participated in more and more trade shows, such as in Bogota in 1953, in Montreal in 1954 and in Lima in 1957, to name but a few. The Crystalworks also prepared for new prospects heralded by the signature of the Treaty of Rome on March 25, 1957 instituting the European Economic

Community. These efforts to redress the situation were rewarded in 1958, on the occasion of the World's Fair in Brussels, where Baccarat was awarded the International First Prize for crystalware. The same year, after twenty years spent as Chairman of the Board of Directors, Jacques Parisot handed over the chairmanship to General de Chambrun who resigned three years later for health reasons. René de Chambrun then became Chairman of the Board, a position he would hold for thirty-two years running during which Baccarat would assert its modernity through its internal operations, the conquest of new markets, and creations, thereby upholding the time-honored principles in force right from the very beginning.

While celebrating its bicentennial in 1964, and already preparing for its tricentennial, Baccarat's craftmanship was honored by an exhibition devoted exclusively to the Company at the Museum of Decorative Arts. A catalog was published for the occasion, in which the curator, Yolande Amic, explains the keys to Baccarat's success in the following terms: "...the taste for restraint, the reason imposed by needs both technical and commercial, caused Baccarat to produce exclusively pieces that are so well designed, of such sure craftmanship, that they withstand the march of time. Far from going out of fashion, the stemware created in the past are timeless as "classic" pieces.

"Massena" stemware

1979

Foundations for the future

In 1964, export sales accounted for 50% of production. Twenty-five years later, they reached 72%. This success was due once again to the fabulous modernization program implemented over the years. Thus in 1967, the Crystalworks was the first European factory to be equipped with a state-of-the-art tank furnace. Initially powered by butane and electricity, then natural gas in 1970, the furnace produced, by continuous fusion, a crystal purer than ever before. A second tank furnace would be fired up in 1976, then a third in 1986.

During this thirty-year period, Baccarat's workforce stabilized at about 1,000 people. On May 1, 1978, a new shareholding structure was established, permitting more than half the employees to become shareholders in the business.

In the 1970's, Baccarat strenghtened its trade relations with Asia. In view of its success, a new company was founded in 1984, *Baccarat Pacific*, based in Tokyo. Five years later, the inauguration of the Kanemori Museum, entirely dedicated to Baccarat, testified to the enthusiasm aroused by the Company. It also confirmed the privileged ties between the Crystalworks and Japan going back to the beginning of the century, when in 1909, a stemware bearing the arms of the Imperial House was ordered from Baccarat.

Glass for the Imperial House of Japan
"Beauvais" stemware, engraved heraldic emblem
1909

Another factor in the success which has lasted over the last thirty years, is the fruitful dialogue between the Crystalworks and its designers. From these exchanges arose works and objects that accentuated changing styles while integrating Baccarat into the world of contemporary design.

Robert Rigot
"Bouquet" stemware for Rhine wine

1971

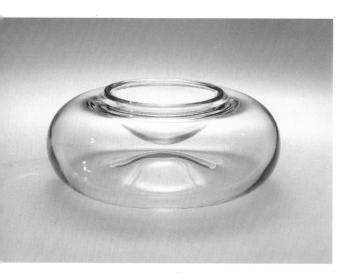

Roberto Sambonet - "Vesuvius" Caviar bowl

1972

Baccarat and its designers

The sixties and seventies

With Emile Gilioli (1911-1977) Baccarat's first abstract sculptures appeared. This association started in 1955 and lasted until 1970.

In 1961, the arrival in Baccarat of a young sculptor, Bernard Augst, allowed the Crystalworks to revive the animal sculptures launched by Georges Chevalier in 1926.

The end of the sixties was marked by Robert Rigot's work. Trained as a sculptor, Rigot created numerous stemware and tableware items. He also designed a series of stylized animal sculptures.

At the beginning of the seventies, Italian designer Roberto Sambonet, brought new life to the Crystalworks. In 1972, he designed a caviar bowl entitled "Vesuvius" playing with the lightness and transparency of the crystal. He repeated this in 1977 with the famous "angle vases." Their precise angular cuts called upon the services of Baccarat's best glassmakers, for they are very difficult to make.

In 1974, collaboration with the designer Van Day Truex generated the creation of the "Dionysos" decanter of timeless simplicity. Salvador Dali who had already lent himself to the play of crystal with his famous perfume bottle "Le Roy Soleil," designed a sculpture thirty years later entitled "Castor and Pollux," inspired by one of his fetish themes: androgeny.

Fruitful collaboration was established in 1973 between Baccarat and the goldsmith Chaumet with the creation of a sumptuous bestiary made with blocks of crystal cut with a burin and adorned with silver, vermeil and precious stones. Some sixty pieces were produced. In 1980, the experience would be repeated with "Zoé" the goose, among others.

The eighties and nineties

In 1982, an exhibition entitled "Contemporary French Glassmakers" organized in the Museum of Decorative Arts in Paris by Yvonne Brunhammer, would bring upheaval to the history of French glass. Consequently, many young glassmakers launched into creation. Some would work with Baccarat, such as Matei Negreanu who designed a "crystal nib" in 1985, or two years later, Yan Zoritchak, with a sculpture entitled "Perseus."

In 1982 as well, another young designer, Thomas Bastide, joined Baccarat. Since then, he has designed numerous stemware such as "Neptune" in 1987,

Van Day Truex - "Dionysos" decanter

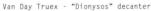
1974

Baccarat & Chaumet - The "Zoe" goose

1980

table pieces, vases and sculptures, including the "Elephant Racines" (1992) which gave new scope to this type of animal art, an integral part of Baccarat's tradition.

The most outstanding designers at the end of the eighties and the beginning of the nineties include Thierry Lecoule, designer of the Versace perfume bottle "V'E Versace' and Nicolas Triboulot who has been designing since 1988 very contemporary shapes, such as the "Vecteur" vase.

The brief collaboration with the designer Eliakim, who passed away in 1992, produced a magnificient fruit bowl.

In 1992, the Argentinian designer Marcial Berro, designed a series of objects. Playing with the "luxury" of crystal, he decorated it with gold droplets, draped with silver and enhanced with "blobs" as an array of luminous cabochons.

Towards the future

In October 1992, new changes took place in Baccarat's destiny. After twenty-two years at the head of the Crystalworks, René de Chambrun resigned leaving the post of Chairman of the Board of Directors to Jean Taittinger, the former Justice Minister and current President of the "Groupe du Louvre", a family-owned business to which he brought an international dimension.

As a stockholder in the Crystalworks since 1988, the "Groupe du Louvre" has provided Baccarat with the necessary resources to tackle the twenty first-century. It is natural that the company, which has survived successive crises and social changes since 1764, is now turning in anticipation towards the future. Strenghtened by its past and its reputation, it is broadening its prospects of modernization brought

by its new Chairman who has followed Baccarat's traditional family past by appointing his daughter, Anne Claire Taittinger-Bonnemaison as managing director of the Crystalworks.

Thomas Bastide - "Elephant Racines"
1992

Thomas Bastide - "Neptune" Stemware

1987

Eliakim - Fruit bowl

1991

Nicolas Triboulot - "Vecteur" vase

1990

Marcial Berro - Champagne bucket

1992

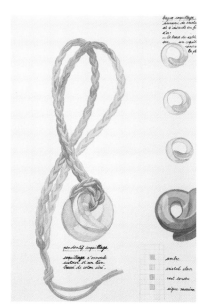

Catherine Noll - "Coquillage" (Shell) series

Patrice Butler

Illustrations of the Future

Jewelry, a new challenge

This field remained unexplored by the Crystalworks until the creation of earrings in 1991. Two years later, Baccarat hired three designers, Evelyne Julienne, Catherine Noll and Thomas Bastide to design the first collection of jewelry.
The glassmakers' art is expressed here in the free flow of the lines and the respect for balancing of shapes, which is proper to Baccarat.

Patrice Butler

In asking this young architect to design a new line of lighting fixtures, Baccarat has revived the splendor of the prestigious chandeliers so admired during the Great Exhibitions of the nineteenth century. Crystal enriched by touches of colors, like an array of precious stones playing with the light, illustrates this modernity in the Baccarat tradition.

3

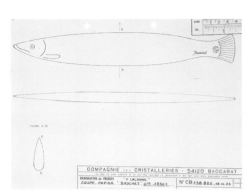

François-Xavier Lalanne - Factory drawing

Andrée Putman

François-Xavier Lalanne

Animals. François-Xavier Lalanne knows them "by
heart." He loves them wholeheartedly, sculpts them,
draws them on metal, paints them on China plates
and gives life to their silhouettes in city
environments. For Baccarat, he had the idea of
"sketching" a crystal barracuda. Paper knife?
Sculpture? Paper knife sculpture?

Andrée Putman

Crystal as an insolent wink, a crystal pendant
suspended like some magnificent unexpected piece
of jewelry lending unexpected luxurious qualities
and a preciousness to a functional object.
Andrée Putman has fun with crystal which she
mixes gracefully with wood and metal in a line of
furniture designed for Baccarat.

to be continued ...

Y. Amic and R. Imbert
*Les presse-papiers français
de cristal, French crystal paperweights,*
Paris, Art et Industrie, 1948.

Y. Amic, *L'opaline française au XIXe
siècle,* Paris, Gründ, 1952.

L'Art du verre, exhibition catalog,
Paris, Musée des Arts Décoratifs, 1951.

Baccarat 1764-1964, exhibition catalog,
Paris, Musée des Arts Décoratifs, 1963.

J. Bellanger, *Verre d'usage
et de prestige France 1500-1800,*
Les Editions de l'Amateur, 1988.

C. Bizot and E. Mannoni,
Mobilier 1900-1925, Paris, Ch. Massin

G. Bontemps, *Guide du verrier,*
Paris, Librairie du dictionnaire des arts
et manufactures, 1868.

A. Brogniart and D. Riocreux,
*Description méthodique du musée
céramique de la manufacture royale
de porcelaine de Sèvres,* Paris, A. Leuleux,
Libraire-Editeur 1845.

Y. Brunhammer, *Le style 1925,*
Paris, Baschet et Cie., 1975.

Y. Brunhammer, "A Baccarat du côté des
flacons", *Baccarat les flacons à parfum,
Répertoire du collectionneur,* Paris,
Compagnie des Cristalleries de Baccarat,
Henri Addor & Associés, 1986, pp. 5-8.

Y. Brunhammer, *Le Beau dans l'Utile,
un musée pour les arts décoratifs,*
Gallimard, 1992.

J.-G. Bulliot, *François-Eugène
de Fontenay,* biographical note,
Autun, Imprimerie Dejussieur, 1886.

J. Carpentier and F. Lebrun,
Histoire de France, Le Seuil, 1987
(revised in 1992).

R. J. Charleston, *Masterpieces of Glass,
a world history from the Corning Museum
of Glass,* New York, Harry N. Abrams Inc.,
1980

J.-L. Curtis and V. Nansenet,
Baccarat, Editions du Regard, 1991.

Didron and Clémandot, *Exposition
Universelle Internationale de 1878 à Paris.*

*Groupe III.-Classe 19. Rapport
sur les cristaux, la verrerie et les vitraux*
Paris, Imprimerie Nationale, 1880.

O. Drahotova, *L'art du verre en Europe,*
Gründ, 1983.

P.-H. Dunlop, *The Jokelson Collection
of Antique Cameo Incrustation,* Phoenix,
Papier Presse, 1991.

Gerspach, *L'art de la verrerie,*
Paris, A. Quentin, Imprimeur-Editeur, 1885.

K. Hettes, *La verrerie en Tchecoslovaquie,*
Maison d'Edition Technique, Prague,
published for the Brussels World Fair, 1958.

G. Ingold, *Les Boules presse-papiers
et les sulfures des cristalleries
de Saint-Louis,* Hermé 1985.

G. Ingold, *Saint-Louis, de l'art du verre à
l'art du cristal de 1586 à nos jours,*
Denoël, 1986.

Le Japonisme, exhibition catalog, Editions
de la Réunion des musées nationaux, 1988.

P. Jokelson and G. Ingold,
Les presse-papiers XIXe et XXe siècles,
Hermé, 1988.

***Le Livre des expositions universelles
1851-1989,*** exhibition catalog
Union Centrale des Arts Décoratifs, 1983.

Marcial Berro, Meubles et Objets,
exhibition catalog, Galerie Pierre
Passebon, Galerie du Passage, 1992.

V. Nansenet, "François-Eugène de
Fontenay, Verrier (1810-1884)". Annals of
the 11th Congress of the Association
Internationale pour l'Histoire du Verre,
Basle, August 28 - September 3, 1988,
Amsterdam, A.I.H.V., 1990.

J.-L. Olivié, "Autour de l'Art Nouveau,"
Cent ans d'art du verre en France,
exhibition catalog, Association
Française d'Action Artistique and Gallery
Hoam du Joong-ang Daily News, Korea,
1986, pp. 29-30.
Ibid., "Art déco et modernisme," pp. 73-74.
Ibid., "Les années 50 et le renouveau du
verre," pp. 108-109.

J.-L. Olivié and S. Petrova, *Verres
de Bohème 1400-1989 Chefs d'oeuvre*

des musées de Tchecoslovaquie,
exhibition catalog, Paris, Musée des Arts
Décoratifs, Flammarion, 1989.

E. Péligot, *Rapport adressé à messieurs
les membres de la Chambre de Commerce
de Paris sur l'exposition des produits de
l'industrie autrichienne, ouverte à Vienne le
15 mai 1845* (Report addressed to members
of the Paris Chamber of Commerce on the
exhibition of products of Austrian industry,
which opened in Vienna on May 15, 1845),
Paris, Imprimerie de Madame Dondey-
Duprey (Widow), January 1846.

E. Péligot, *Rapport du XXIVe Jury, verres
et cristaux,* (Report by the 24th Jury for
glass and ceramics), Great Exhibition of
London 1851, Paris, 1854.

E. Péligot., *Le verre, son histoire, sa
fabrication,* Paris, G. Masson, Editeur, 1877.

A. Plessis, *De la fête impériale au mur des
fédérés 1852-1871,* Nouvelle Histoire de
la France contemporaine 9, Le Seuil, 1979.

R. Rémond, *Le XIX siècle 1815-1914
Introduction à l'histoire de notre temps 2,*
Le Seuil, 1974.

F. Renaud, *La cristallerie de Baccarat
de ses origines à la fin du XIX siècle,*
Thesis submitted to the Faculty of
Letters of Nancy for the Diplôme d'Etudes
Supérieures d'Histoire, October 1947.

F.-O. Rousseau, *Andrée Putman,* Paris,
Editions du Regard, 1989.

J.-P. Rioux, *La révolution industrielle
1780-1880,* Le Seuil, 1971 and 1989.

A. Sauzay, *La verrerie depuis les temps
les plus reculés jusqu'à nos jours,*
Bibliothèque des merveilles, Paris,
Hachette, 1869.

J. Shadel Spillman, *Glass from World's
Fairs 1851-1904,* Corning, New York,
The Corning Museum of Glass, 1986.

***Transparences, l'art du verre en France
de 1914 à 1960,*** exhibition catalog,
Musée des Beaux Arts d'Orléans, 1987.

***Verriers Français Contemporains
Art et Industrie,*** exhibition catalog,
Paris, Musée des Arts Décoratifs, 1982.

Acknowledgements

We would like to express our gratitude to Jean-Luc Olivié, Curator of the Glass Center, Museum of Decorative Arts, Paris, and Anne Vanlatum, head of documentation at the Glass Center, Museum of Decorative Arts, Paris, for the invaluable help they gave to make this book possible.

Photo credits:

Jacques Boulay

Laurent Sully-Jaulmes

Baccarat Archives

Studio Kollar

Graphic Design

LM communiquer

Layout

Beau fixe

Plouguerneau

Lady Baccarat

1964

Created in 1964 for the Exhibition of the Bicentennial of Baccarat at the Museum of Decorative Arts in Paris.